Indian Business Case Studies

Indian Business Case Studies

Volume I

SANDEEP PACHPANDE
ASHA PACHPANDE
J A KULKARNI

Indian Case Studies in Business Management

OXFORD
UNIVERSITY PRESS

Great Clarendon Street, Oxford, ox2 6dp,
United Kingdom

Oxford University Press is a department of the University of Oxford.
It furthers the University's objective of excellence in research, scholarship,
and education by publishing worldwide. Oxford is a registered trade mark of
Oxford University Press in the UK and in certain other countries

Published in the United States of America by Oxford University Press
198 Madison Avenue, New York, NY 10016, United States of America

British Library Cataloguing in Publication Data

Data available

Library of Congress Cataloging-in-Publication Data: 2022938091

ISBN 978–0–19–286937–1

DOI: 10.1093/oso/9780192869371.001.0001

Dr R.R. Pachpande
[1947–2009]

'Education is the Soul of our society.'

The series editors and the volume authors of the case volumes titled as
'Indian Business Case Studies' published by Oxford University Press have
a deep sense of gratefulness while dedicating these case volumes to the
memory of Dr Raghunath R. Pachpande, the founder of ASM Group of
Institutes Pune, India.

It was with the untiring efforts and strategic vision of Dr R.R. (as he was
known to his close friends and colleagues) which has been instrumental in
ASM group adopting case methodology as a unique element in its pedagogy
which motivated the faculty and students of ASM group of institutes to
develop business case studies on Indian businesses and use them to teach
management subjects in all branches of business management studies.

Dr R.R. Pachpande was a leader beyond parlance and ahead of time in
establishing educational institutes more so in higher studies in business
management specifically in the industrial belts in the state of Maharashtra
with a view to providing best of experiential learning to its students
through closer interactions with business units around.

Today ASM group continues the great legacy of Dr R.R. Pachpande under the leadership of his successors and who have succeeded in taking ASM group to global recognition as a unique group of institutes offering world-class education in all branches of business management.

This case volume is dedicated to the memories of late Dr R.R. Pachpande.

Contents

SECTION II CASE STUDIES IN FINANCE MANAGEMENT

Preface

Many universities and management institutes across the globe have adopted the case study methodology for teaching almost all branches of management studies since several decades. This trend has been seen in India also, wherein the Indian Institutes of Management (IIMs) and progressive management institutes in private sector have implemented case methodology as an important pedagogical tool in business management education.

However, there is a severe shortage in Indian business case studies faced by the B-schools in India and those global institutes associated with Indian academia. Majority of the case studies studied at IIMs and other A-grade B-schools in India are from situations in industries in foreign countries and have very little or no relevance to Indian business situations. This acts as a major gap for faculty and students engagement in business management studies both at UG and masters level (PG) studies, wherein clarification of theoretical concepts is possible mainly through use of case methodology which enables insight into business real-life business situations.

Besides, the objectives and purposes for which case studies are developed abroad are much different from course of studies in Indian B-schools. Therefore, the dependence on foreign case studies for Indian students does not provide any real situational insight on Indian business. Although the curriculum requires taking the students through case study methodology, there are not many Indian case studies for this purpose.

Acknowledgements

The series editors wish to acknowledge with thanks to the contribution of data for the case studies from ASM's Academic Associates the CETYS University Mexico—Dr Scott Venezia, Dean International Affairs, and Dr Faviola Villegas Prof in marketing for case studies on Hyundai-Kia and McDonalds as also several senior faculties from ASM Group of Institutes for their help in proofreading and editing of the case studies.

We also acknowledge the numerous news reporters of daily newspapers in business and economics in India which have been rich and authentic secondary data sources for design and development of case studies for the case volumes.

About the Series Editors

Dr Sandeep Pachpande, Chairman
ASM Group of Institutes, Pune, India

Prof J.A. Kulkarni,
Professor, ASM Group of Institutes, Pune, India

Both the series editors have decades of experience in business case design and development as also implementation of case methodology of teaching for the faculty and students of business schools in India and abroad.

The series editors have to give their credit for authoring three major books on business case studies published by globally known publishers and in conducting workshops for case design and development

The series editors have a very good network with leaders and stalwarts in business management studies across the globe and are popular as keynote speakers in many national and international conferences. They have a very rich experience in organizing national and international conferences and case competitions.

Currently the series editors are busy in completing a unique case analysis and resolution methodology programme which is under copyright considerations.

Dr Sandeep Pachpande   **Prof J. A. Kulkarni**

About the Volume Authors

Dr Sandeep Pachpande

Chairman, ASM Group of Institutes Pune, India

An academician, entrepreneur, real estate developer, technopreneur, mentor, author, keynote speaker, agriculturist, and visionary Dr Sandeep Pachpande brings a multi-faceted business sense to the table every day. With a vision to provide global standards of education combined with the strength of industry exposure, binds his avid leadership that has guided and mentored careers of thousands of students.

A Computer Engineer, Dr Sandeep Pachpande is Harvard Business School alumni and done executive programmes from Kellogg, Babson, and is Gold Medallist in MBA from Leeds Metropolitan University, UK. He is a PhD guide, keynote speaker, has authored many books, and has travelled to 36 countries on various assignments, conferences, seminars, study tours, and delegations and is truly global in his thought, words, and deeds.

Prof J.A. Kulkarni

Prof. J.A. Kulkarni brings along with him nearly 40 years of industry experience at senior levels including Tata Motors, M&M Ltd., and Bajaj Auto Ltd. He is a University Gold Medallist for his BE in Mech Engineering and backed up by a post-graduate education in management from Germany.

Prof. Kulkarni during his 16 years of experience with ASM Group of Institutes specializes in teaching MBA students in subjects such as Strategic Management and Sustainability.

Prof. Kulkarni's major contribution has been in the development of a unique case resolution method and in the development of several business case studies. He has authored book on business case studies and also on innovative management, and contributed more than 25 research papers for national and international conferences. Prof. Kulkarni has visited several countries on business negotiations and also as visiting faculty on a few of the foreign universities. Prof. J.A. Kulkarni is nominated as Board of ISODC USA as International Director and has participated in several international conferences and organizing workshops/conferences and case competitions.

Dr Asha Pachpande

As Founder Secretary and Director of ASM, Dr Asha Pachpande is firmly committed to her belief that education goes beyond a certificate and is more about its implementation in real-world business scenarios. For this purpose she went about building a strong industry-institute connect which benefitted the students of ASM from the employability and career prospects. She is a staunch supporter of use of case methodology as a part of ASM group's pedagogy.

She has travelled extensively in India and abroad to countries like Japan, Germany, France, Hong Kong, Thailand, U.K., and U.S.A. to attend national and international seminars and conferences. She has worked on many important positions as an advisor and guide at the university and state-level management associations.

As an educationist she has been recognized at the highest forums and is the recipient of many prestigious awards like Savitribai Phule STREE RATNA PURASKAR and Life Time Achievement Award 2019 by CEGR India to name a few.

A Teaser for the Readers

Why Focus on Indian Business Case Studies?

Business case studies on Indian business environment

The Crux of the Issues

Business case studies and their relevance to management education
Many B-schools outside India have adopted decades ago the case study methodology for teaching almost all branches of management studies. This trend has been seen in India also, wherein a majority of the Indian Institutes of Management (IIMs) have implemented case study-based methodology as an important pedagogical tool in business management education. The major issue in India is, however, the inadequate interaction between B-schools and industries. The fault lies with both B-schools and the industry. The B-schools in a majority of cases cannot provide research-based solutions to industry problems due to a lack of necessary infrastructure and facilities. And the industries in the absence of any direct benefit from the institutes are not inclined to waste their time and funds on B-school education.

Hence, there is a severe shortage in Indian case studies through which the B-schools can provide industry insight to its students. Majority of the case studies studied at IIMs and other A-grade B-schools are imported from abroad. These case studies are from situations in industries in foreign countries and have very little or no relevance to Indian students who have to necessarily study the situations in Indian industries.

Besides, the objectives and purposes for which case studies are developed abroad are much different from the level and course of studies in Indian B-schools. Therefore, the dependence on foreign case studies for Indian students does not provide any real situational insight on Indian business. Although the syllabus for management studies requires taking the students through case study methodology, unfortunately, there are not many Indian case studies that can be discussed with the students.

Thus, it is a Catch-22 situation. Unless institutes have the capability and the required infrastructure to cater to industry-related issues, they cannot expect any interactive support from the industries; unless institutes get adequate data from industries, their teaching content and quality continue to be much less than the expectations of the industry from students who pass out from such institutes.

This is not specific to Indian environment alone the same situation more or less is prevalent in most of the developed countries as well.

Objectives of Use of Case Study Methodology

The main objectives of using case-based teaching as a major pedagogical tool in B-schools are as follows:

1. To facilitate students' concept development capabilities through exposure to real-life problems in industries.
2. To enable students to correlate theoretical topics with the techniques used in analysing complex issues in business situations.
3. To develop skills using which students can develop application matrix for the theoretical topics for real-life problem analysis and resolution techniques.
4. Help the students of B-schools to develop orientation towards the important attributes and attitudinal requirements for effective handling of complex situations at the workplace.
5. To develop a clear understanding of the techniques used for problem analysis, situation analysis, and decision analysis and appropriate understanding of the difference between problems and situations in management.
6. To develop the group-based approaches to solving problems and challenges at the workplace by appropriate coordination of and collaboration with all related aspects of a situation.
7. To develop a reference manual for recording the problems tackled and the essential lessons learnt from past incidences for use in future eventualities of recurrence of issues.

8. To develop the preventive steps that must be initiated to ensure the problems resolved once do not recur in the immediate future.

Types of Case Studies

The entire gamut of business case studies can be classified as follows:

1. Evaluative case studies—Teaching case
2. Task- or action-oriented case studies (including project-based case studies)
3. Research-oriented case studies—Case research

Teaching case studies are basically oriented towards developing the evaluative and analytical skills of students towards industry situations. Such case studies draw the attention of participants of the case resolution methodology on the in-depth correlative evaluation of the issues in the case study with the various related topics that the students have to study about in their classrooms. These case studies could be on issues related to human resources, industrial relations, product and process, marketing and finance management areas in business management.

Such case studies help the students mainly to examine their understanding of evaluative steps such as evaluation of the financial situation of a company or the quality aspects of its products and services, etc. The task- or action-oriented case studies dwell on business issues that call for appropriate decision-making capabilities of executives. By involving students of management studies in the resolution activity of such case studies, the skills learnt by them through the theoretical studies can be experimented in the resolution exercises.

The students can be motivated to apply their decision-making skills along with their risk management ability to make business decisions. Developing a plan of actions oriented towards the resolution of the case issues calls for effective role-play techniques as also presentation skills from the part of students; they are normally required to defend their plan of approach and decisions in front of other students and the faculty, which helps them improve their capabilities to sustain questions and criticisms, normal features in business management.

Research-based case studies, as the name suggests, involve students in research initiatives to establish a hypothesis or to disprove a common belief, which influences the progress and sustenance of business ideologies or even scientific or technical aspects of business dynamics. These case studies normally call for prerequisites such as thorough business knowledge and enough exposure to both the theoretical and practical aspects of the issues presented in the case studies. Issues of corporate governance and social welfare functions, which have both obligatory and voluntary elements attached to them, are pursued in research studies to establish the utility purposes of such aspects, which range from free will to a compelled activity.

However, the real problem today for B-schools is the non-availability of good case studies on Indian business. Recently, it was reported that IIMs (IIM Bangalore) are resorting to appointing consultants to develop case studies on Indian enterprises, since the usage of imported case studies from foreign businesses is fast losing its relevance to the Indian business scenario, which in itself has unique features among the global economies. India, which is rated as the world's fourth-largest economy, definitely needs specific and separate approaches to the case study methodology as a pedagogical tool for B-school studies.

The Present Environment

The academic environment across the world is facing a major disruption on account of the global pandemic Covid-19 forcing the offline education to switch over to online/blended versions of teaching and learning process. And use of case methodology and simulation exercises are the main ingredients while maintaining the effective ways of delivering experiential learning through the use of case and case lets in an online mode of teaching ensuring student engagements and online interactive ways of knowledge dissemination. Realizing this requirement even globally reputed institutes such as Harvard and MIT Sloan have made case method of teaching an essential part of their online courses.

ASM group with nearly 250 business case studies developed by its faculty over years takes pleasure in offering these cases mostly on Indian businesses through these case volumes to the faculty, students, and also for executive education programmes. The case studies are selected from ASM's captive case bank as most appropriate for the current day syllabi and on Indian business scenario including select live case studies on ongoing businesses.

The case volumes also have few cases on foreign business situations basically to provide a bit of variety and correlation of issues across the globe.

The series editors and the volume authors of this volume along with ASM Group of Institutes Pune, India are certain that the case volumes as published will receive excellent response from the faculty and students alike in B-schools in India and abroad.

SECTION I

CASE STUDIES IN HUMAN RESOURCES

HR, Entrepreneurship, CSR, CG, and Sustainability

1

'Managing Business with Respect'

A Case Study on ITC-triple Bottom Line Approach

Learning Objectives

To identify, evaluate, and develop marketing strategies of ITC in India. To evaluate business sustainability and competitive advantages. To detect the cross-industry variation in the strategic orientation. To assess the focus of selected organizations on individual variants of strategic management viz. strategic intent, strategic formulation, strategic implementation, and strategic control. To detect the loopholes in the strategic orientation of the ITC which might have retarded their operating efficiency. To give some practicable suggestions to the selected large organizations so that these may make necessary changes in their strategic outlook for competitive advantage.

Synopsis

The ITC company was incorporated in 1910. Much has changed in these 100 years. ITC itself has metamorphosed in many ways, the least of which is the multiple changes in nomenclature. What began and stayed for long as only a cigarette maker has turned into a conglomerate offering a dashboard of products and services, ranging from hospitality to toiletry to apparel to food. Of course, cigarettes remain a big but gradually shrinking part of its overall business.

Indian Business Case Studies. Sandeep Pachpande, Asha Pachpande, and J A Kulkarni, Oxford University Press.
© ASM Group of Institutes, Pune, India 2022. DOI: 10.1093/oso/9780192869371.003.0001

ITC had a market cap of over Rs 100,000 crore and ended 2008–2009 with a turnover of Rs 15,582 crore. It employs over 26,000 people at more than 60 locations across India and has 338,000 shareholders. It is but one of the scores of India's centurion companies. Among others, Andrew Yule is alive and kicking even at 130 years of age. Then there are Allahabad Bank, Walchandnagar Industries, Tata Steel, Bank of Baroda, Indian Bank, Alembic, Corporation Bank, Canara Bank, Bank of India, Shalimar Paints, Indian Hotels, Spencer & Company, Century Textiles, Punjab National Bank, and Bombay Dyeing. Many companies were originally British and became Indian through the fifties, sixties, and seventies. There are many that assumed Indian names after takeovers by home-grown business houses.

Originally incorporated as Imperial Tobacco Company of India, ITC too has undergone a few name changes. As its ownership became largely Indian, it became India Tobacco Company in 1970. Then, keeping in fashion of the day, it abbreviated itself to ITC in 1974. That was in recognition of its changing business portfolio, which by then included hotels. Later it was to add information technology, packaging, paperboards and speciality papers, agricultural business, foods, lifestyle retailing, education and stationery products, personal care, and clothing.

Very few Indian companies have reinvented themselves as ITC has. Realizing long ago that cigarette cannot be its bread and butter for long, given the rising campaign against smoking, the company first moved into hotels and then into the FMCG business—both have brought handsome rewards. Even in organizational matters, it has brought about vast changes. For example, its divisional CEOs run their businesses almost independently; yet there's a high level of synergy across those businesses.

Much of the change has come about under the stewardship of chairman YC Deveshwar, who has adopted a three-pronged strategy to continue growth in the years to come. As ITC officials say the strategy is to 'emerge as a sustainable company with national priorities and further Indians capital and resources.'

ITC and Its Business Ideology

'The company will increasingly focus on volume-based businesses and areas with the highest scope for direct interface with customers. It will strive to turn as many brands as possible into market leaders', officials in the know say.

'It is the right move at the right time, the company could survive and grow for so long simply because of its professional management and thrust on training and retraining of employees. One of every seven employees is sent for extensive training and, if need be, re-training. As the company reinvents itself, its employees are also re-trained.'

The company's transformation started in 1968 was not easy or smooth. 'ITC's overseas shareholders were only interested in the tobacco business. ITC had to convince them so that they stay invested in the company. Dealing with the government on various approval-related issues was not easy either.'

The former vice-chairman and director of corporate strategies of ITC said the recent strategies had been working wonders for the company. 'We have all along stayed away from very high tech areas. Over the years, the company has concentrated on—and should continue to concentrate on—socially relevant areas, where there are volumes and higher customer contacts like hotel, paper, etc., and areas where the company can leverage its proverbial distribution network.'

For six decades after its inception, the focus was solely on cigarettes and leaf tobacco business; the seventies saw the beginnings of a corporate transformation. According to its website, the company's diversified status originates from its corporate strategy aimed at creating multiple drivers of growth anchored on distribution reach, brand-building, effective supply chain management, and service skills in the hotel business.

The packaging and printing business was set up in 1925 as a strategic backward integration for the cigarettes business. The hotel business was started in 1975 with the acquisition of a hotel in Chennai. The property was later rechristened ITC-WelcomeGroup. Today, the company has over 100 owned and managed properties spread across India.

In 1979 ITC entered the paperboards business by promoting ITC Bhadrachalam Paperboards, which today has become the market leader in India. Bhadrachalam Paperboards amalgamated with ITC in March 2002 and became a division. In November the same year this division merged with the company's Tribeni Tissues division to form the paperboards and speciality papers division.

In 1990, leveraging its sourcing competency, ITC set up the agricultural business division for the export of commodities. The division is today one of India's largest exporters. Ten years later, it started what was then unique and by now widely acknowledged e-copal initiative with soya farmers in Madhya Pradesh. Now it extends to 10 states covering over four million farmers.

Also in 2000 ITC forayed into the greeting, gifting, and stationery product business with the launch of the 'Expressions' range of greeting cards. A line of premium range of notebooks under the Paper Kraft brand was launched in 2002. A year later, it launched the 'Classmate' brand of notebooks to reach a wider body of students. It is now India's biggest notebook brand which includes school bags. Between 2007 and 2009, it launched children's books, geometry boxes, pens, and pencils too. Lifestyle retailing was embraced in 2000 with the Wills Sport range for men and women. Within two years it widened its portfolio with the men's wear brand, John Players. The information technology business was turned into a wholly owned subsidiary, ITC InfoTech India, in 2000.

ITC stepped into the foods business in 2001 with a range of ready-to-eat Indian gourmet dishes under the Kitchens of India brand. Then came the confectionery and staples segments with Mint-O and Candyman and Aashirvaad atta (wheat flour). Sunfeast biscuits followed quickly.

The next move was a logical extension of the food business. Bingo, the snack brand, came in 2007. In eight years, the foods business has grown significantly, with over 200 differentiated products under six distinctive brands. Among other products launched in the past eight years are safety matches and agarbattis, the latter in partnership with the cottage sector. In toiletry, ITC's Fiama Di Wills, a premium range of shampoos, shower gels, and soaps came in quick succession in the last four months of 2007. Around the same time, the mass market and shampoos were introduced. The higher-end Vivel de Wills and Vivel range of soaps and shampoos came in 2008.

ITC has made a successful transition from being a cigarettes company to a consumer goods seller in the past two years. Its consumer goods portfolio, today, includes soaps, shampoos, biscuits, and salty snacks among others.

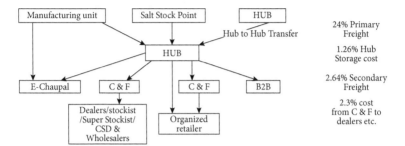

ITC Distribution Strategy

These are all extremely competitive consumer categories with well-entrenched multinational as well as domestic players such as Hindustan Unilever, Procter & Gamble, Dabur, and Marico. With the right product and marketing mix, ITC has not only managed to create a space for itself in this overly crowded consumer segment but has built a strong brand recall as well among its target consumers. In 2009, the company launched variants of its popular salty snack brand Bingo! Chips. The launch was well supported by a brilliant advertising campaign that won consumers' attention as well as immense creative applaud.

Starting with the first of the Bingo! Commercials, which showed scientists falling over themselves in selecting the best of three identical triangles, aka Bingo! Mad Angles, the ads have continued with their irreverent and humorous messaging. The latest are its Bingo! Red Chilli Bijli and Bingo! International Cream and Onion Potato variants, which have helped the brand cater to every palate.

At a time when most rivals were reeling under tremendous cost pressures and depressed consumer demand, the company has registered impressive results on the back of a good product mix, smart sourcing of raw materials, and several cost management steps. Its non-cigarette FMCG segment continued to improve on profitability while revenues from the sector grew 14% in the July–September 2009 quarter. Investments in brand building in the FMCG segment have also brought in handsome results. Higher taxes notwithstanding, cigarette sales grew impressively and so did the rural agri-business.

The company says its the focus on innovation and specific consumer needs that has enabled its business to deliver superior value. A well-crafted portfolio of brands with a good blend of contemporary packaging and marketing communication is the other secret to its success.

Water-positive and carbon-positive, India's largest cigarette maker ITC is known almost as much for its other activities now. It has earned it new respect, and fuelled growth at a time when the core business is facing limitations.

That is what ITC has accomplished through decades of focus on sustainability and corporate social responsibility (CSR). In fact, it has achieved the near-impossible of diverting attention away from its core business of tobacco, which pooled in 48% of its turnover some years ago.

'For six years in a row, ITC has been a water-positive company, and for three consecutive years to date, we have sustained our carbon-positive status, notwithstanding the large growth in our business. Today, we have three times more fresh water harvesting potential than what we consume and sequester almost twice the amount of carbon we emit. This year, we have also achieved the 100 per cent benchmark in recycling solid waste in several of our operations. This makes us the only company in the world, of our size and diversity, to have achieved these three milestones,' said Yogi C Deveshwar, the company's ex-chairman.

The journey to these milestones has been paved by several gallons of midnight oil burnt by ITC executives to resolve tricky issues. In hotels, for instance, the challenge lies in disposal of food from the kitchen, and of the old linen and towels that pile up in the store. The solutions are innovative—tying up with piggeries to utilize food fit for animal consumption and converting the rest into compost to be used as manure. The linen and towels are given away to orphanages. Leftover ghee and oil in the kitchens are transported to a soap factory to be used as raw material.

The challenges were the biggest for ITC's Bhadrachalam paperboard plant, which generates enormous solid waste. The fly ash generated from the boilers in the mill is used to make bricks. And to demonstrate that the fly ash bricks are as durable as their more conventional counterparts, they have been used by the company to build its own staff colony.

Agriculture Entrance of ITC: e-Choupal

Today, the company has 6,500 e-Choupals (internet-driven knowledge kiosks that give farmers information and services for all aspects of farming) covering 40,000 villages and over 4 million farmers, and a social forestry initiative that has greened over 80,000 hectares and created 35 million man-days of employment.

For long a force in the hospitality sector (Maurya), it has become a major player in the areas of apparel (Wills Lifestyle) and foods (Sunfeast, Aashirvaad, Kitchens of India). When it comes to public perception, these have become as prominent, if not more, than ITC's cigarette brands, which do not make for a happy discussion at public forums and whose advertising avenues are restricted by law. Still, the fact is that the company pays its bills and its shareholders with tobacco money. Many of the new businesses, funded by the earnings from tobacco, have yet to stop being a drain on the resources.

That raises the uncomfortable question: does this whole thing amount so far too little more than a corporate social responsibility, or CSR, initiative to make people stop linking ITC to tobacco? Or is there deep strategic thinking behind it? The answer is complexity's diversification thrust started early with forays into paper manufacturing, deep-sea fishing, and hospitality ventures. But it's only recently, after more than 35 years of sustained efforts—that ITC has come to be seen as an entity that creates value for both stakeholders and society at large. With the launch of e-Choupals in 2000, ITC took a bold step towards aligning its business goals with the empowerment of farmers and help farmers get real-time access to farming knowledge, weather information, and transparent price comparisons.

When ITC diversified into packaged foods with the launch of the 'Kitchens of India' brand in 2001, e-Choupal provided the confidence of a bolstered supply chain. 'The cost-efficient sourcing and identity-preservation of raw agri-materials such as wheat and potato have been the key factors for the rapid success of ITC's branded foods business.'

Potatoes form a large part of its snack foods business, while wheat supply is critical for packaged wheat flour. No less than a million tons of wheat is sourced through e-Choupals to replenish its thriving wheat flour brand, Aashirvaad. Launched in 2002, Aashirvaad has already left its closest rival, Hindustan Unilever's Annapurna, behind and appropriated over 50% of the market for itself. The subtle, unadvertised regional cus-tomization in the atta's composition has worked to make it the preferred brand. The ease with which ITC can interact with farmers, thanks to e-Choupal's backward integration, has enabled the company to get the right crop mix of wheat varieties to cater to different regional palates. The last but vital task of mixing and churning the wheat flour, so it gets cooked the way home-makers want, is ensured by the company's legacy of blending tobacco. The wheat supply has not only helped Aashirvaad lord it over the branded atta market, it has also provided the dough for its line of biscuits, whose sales, according to market estimates, scaled Rs 700 crore in 2006, when market leader Britannia's turnover was Rs 1,500 crore.

e-Choupals have armed ITC with a rural retail network that has organ-ized retailers queuing up to tap it. For every 40 e-Choupals, ITC has one ChoupalSagar a physical marketing hub where farmers can get hands-on training, hire a tractor, or just shop for FMCGs and durables. The next couple of years witnessed ITC managing the back-end operations logis-tics, warehousing, and stores of the likes of Food Bazaar and India Bulls Marts, leveraging its ChoupalSagar experience.

Much before e-Choupal captured the popular imagination, ITC was working with marginal farmers as part of its paperboards business. The association, however, was borne as much out of necessity as intent. Bhadrachalam Paperboards Ltd, set up in Andhra Pradesh in 1975, which later merged with the parent company in 2001 to form ITC's paperboards and speciality papers division, ventured into farm forestry in the early 1980s, when government regulations made it tough to source raw ma-terial from the forests located around the establishment.

The challenge lay in finding an alternative source of wood pulp that would not resort to imports and one that would be faster than the erst-while seven years of plant maturing. The company hit upon a plan that would not only ensure a steady supply of raw materials but also provide year-around jobs to farmers. It tied up with small and marginal farmers of the region who would raise fast-growing plantations for the factory. The idea saw wastelands growing pulpwood plantations that yielded three times more pulp and supplied 90% of the woody raw material that kept the huge Bhadrachalam machines rolling.

Today, with access to 80,000 hectares, ITC has become one of the first carbon-positive corporations of its size and complexity in the world. As many as 13,492 households in 406 villages are earning more than their seasonal farming wages. So successful has ITC's paperboards business been, the company claims, that it consumes just 20% of the over 4,70,000 tons per annum of manufactured paperboards it produces, with the rest meeting the demand of other companies. The business has clocked a profit of Rs 124 crore (an increase of 43% year-on-year) supplying to other corporations and ITC's own businesses that involve packaging for its food, tobacco, and personal care products.

For ITC, starting to do good for society couldn't have come at a better time. Much of it coincided with the government's clamping down on tobacco products and anti-smoking legislation being passed. ITC ran the risk of being saddled with a primary business that could only gain stronger pejorative shades: cigarettes. The anti-tobacco lobby, often training its guns on the cigarette industry, was backed by the government when it amended the Cable TV Act in 1995, culminating in the ministry of information and broadcasting banning cigarette advertisements in 2000. Even surrogate advertising was banned in 2002. The company, of course, could still have done without advertisements, backed as it was with nearly a decade-old legacy and a distribution reach few Indian companies could boast of. But the clampdown has seeped into the government's taxation patterns as well, and ITC, like its peers, felt the heat.

With the mounting taxes—from excise duties to value-added tax—the company could not miss the negative vibes. It was only a matter of time before the rising tax burden eroded ITC's robust revenues from the Rs 6,635 crore cigarette business (FY08 estimates) for a capital employed of Rs 2314.64 crore (that powers all its new ventures). The ever-increasing tax levies have shrunk the cigarette market as well, with many downgrading to low-cost but more harmful tobacco options such as khaini and gutkha.

Paperboards and foods are perhaps the first two in a series of businesses to come supported by ITC's sustainability efforts. For example, the livestock development programme a part of ITC's 'SunheraKal' project, which has started to supplement those families which are in the immediate catchment areas of their factories (in Munger, Bihar, for instance) may one day equip ITC with the resources for dairy farming.

ITC had not expanded into new businesses and stayed with just cigarettes, the top lines growth would have come much slower. There has been a paradigm shift in diversification under the leadership of Deveshwar. 'With the accelerated growth, the new businesses, especially the non-cigarette FMCG portfolio, account for over 50 per cent of our turnover. It has been a strategic decision to grow through FMCG.' Most of the ITC FMCG divisions already have 8 to 10 per cent of the market, and lead in the Attamarket. 'Some of ITC's businesses have exhibited enviable speed, with the snacks brand 'Bingo' reportedly securing 11 per cent of the market within six months of its launch in 2007. ITC claims a market share of 40–45 per cent in the packaged food market and almost 12 per cent in snacks.'

The company knows that in the long run, consumers, especially the business-to-business ones, will settle for an environmentally conscious company. The business customers prefer the carbon-neutrality in ITC's packaging and paper businesses, which are produced through the elemental-chlorine-free technology that is kind to the environment. 'When we talk to international customers such as Wal-Mart, they question us on sustainability, which has now become a qualifier': 'The awareness of what the company does today is much higher than in our time. I think ITC is now respected even more', says a company executive.

ITC has carefully reduced the presence of the cigarette business and focusing much more on its fresh ventures and achievements as a corporate citizen. A clever re-branding has taken the Wills brand's association much beyond cigarettes, so that the equity built over the decades because of ITC's dominance of the cigarette market is reaped by other products like apparel. While cigarettes generated Rs 961.41 crore in profits in the first quarter of 2009, the non-tobacco FMCG products eroded Rs 122.61 crore. The hotels, agri-business, and paperboards and packaging have registered year-on-year growth rates ranging from 33 to 43%. The new business of readymade clothing retail, too, is making dents in ITC's profit.

But ITC's socially relevant programmes will come to its rescue to support the gestation of new businesses. ITC's exports continue to strengthen farmers, who are its key suppliers, the spread of ChoupalSagars has ensured that the company's FMCG products (except for the high-end) are within reach of the rural population. So there, a whole new yardstick now measures the work done in ITC's offices and in the outfields, compelling the rest of the world to take a whole new view

ITC Forges in Sustainable Business Models Focused on Rural India

ITC Schemes

- e-Choupal initiative is designed to enhance farm productivity and provide market linkages.
- Social forestry scheme has greened over 80,000 hectares.
- R&D projects have evolved high-yielding, site-specific, disease-resistant clones.
- Comprehensive package of plantation management practices.
- Watershed development projects benefit 33,311 farmers in 24 districts.

In an increasingly inter-connected world, stakeholders including investors and consumers have raised the bar of expectations from private sector in terms of their response to issues of ethics, transparency, and sustainability concerns.

e-Choupal

ITC's e-Choupal initiative designed to enhance farm productivity and provide market linkages and numbering 6,500, cover 40,000 villages, and benefit over 4 million farmers.

Social Forestry

The social forestry initiative of the company has greened over 80,000 hectares and created cumulative employment of 35 million man-days, besides providing a reliable source of wood pulp for the long-term competitiveness and sustainability of ITC's paper business.

Plantation Management

Over 93% of the company's Bhadrachalam mill's aggregate wood need in 2007–2008 came from plantations initiated through the forestry project undertaken by tribal and marginal farmers. As the availability of wood, the prime source of fibre for the paper and paperboards remains a key challenge and concern for sustainability, the company's R&D initiatives have evolved high-yielding, disease-resistant clones, and a comprehensive package of plantation management practices.

The sustainability report said the company is committed to green one lakh hectares in the next few years, which would far exceed its wood fibre requirement, foster livelihood chances for a very large number of people in tribal belts, and further consolidate its position as a 'carbon positive' corporation.

Renewable Energy

What is particularly noteworthy is that 96% of the company's energy requirements are panned out internally with more than 24% of energy generated from renewable resources.

The report also highlights that ITC has been a 'water positive' firm and today the company generates three times more freshwater harvesting potential than it consumes and sequesters almost twice the amount of carbon its plants emit.

Recycling Solid Waste

In 2007–2008, the company also compassed the 100% benchmark in recycling solid waste in several of its operations. Moreover, the company's watershed development projects now assist farmers in 24 districts, benefiting 33,311 farmers. A total of 2,178 water harvesting structures have been created, providing critical irrigation to 18,483 hectares of farmland.

Finally, ITC's 'Mission SunehraKal' encompassing its sustainable development initiatives would continue to provide thrust to identified triple interventions viz., natural resource management (wasteland, watershed, and agriculture development); sustainable livelihoods comprising genetic improvement in livestock; and economic empowerment of women and community development with focus on primary education, health, and sanitation.

Social policy analysts contend that if CSR is taken by all big companies earnestly with a view to building public-private partnership for sustainable and inclusive growth, the simmering tensions and resistance to industrial development through setting up economic enclaves or big projects would gradually fade as rural people would hopefully find a decent way out of their dire predicament of penury of the company.

WOW—Wealth Out of Waste

ITC has decided to step up its waste paper collection business under its WOW (Wealth out of Waste) programme, to augment raw material supply for its paperboard mills. ITC uses about 1.8 lakh tons of imported waste paper annually at its mills in Coimbatore and Bhadrachalam. According to company officials, it needs about 3 lakh tons of waste paper annually. The balance is sourced domestically. The company views the WOW programme as an opportunity to step up domestic raw material availability.

As part of the programme, now on in the four southern states, it has tied up with Ramky Infrastructure to launch door-to-door domestic waste collection. The company takes the paper-based materials for its own use and the other waste is recycled through tie-ups with other recyclers. According to Mr B. Joga Rao, vice-president (Commercial), ITC (Paperboards and Specialty Papers Division), the company now collects about 3,000 tons of waste paper a month, through the WOW programme. It plans to increase collection to about 5,000 tons a month in April, and by the year end, to about 10,000 tons.

WOW is now on in five cities including Hyderabad and Visakhapatnam in Andhra Pradesh; Chennai, Coimbatore, and Madurai in Tamil Nadu; Bangalore and Kochi.

The company plans to extend the programme to other cities and is targeting educational institutions as well. In Hyderabad, it has implemented the programme in seven schools and plans to launch it in twenty-five more. Children will be taught the value of recycling—one ton of paper produced from recycled material saves 22 trees, he said.

As countries across the globe increase recycling of waste paper for conservation needs and cost benefits, Indian paper manufacturers, who depend on imported waste paper, are increasingly feeling the pinch of waste paper shortage and increasing costs. According to ITC officials, the price of waste paper had increased by 30–40% in the last three months to around Rs 9,000–9,500 a ton. ITC has also tied up with around 100 companies to procure their waste paper.

Imported waste paper prices have been spiralling, as developed countries and major producers such as China are cutting back on virgin wood for paper production and increasing the use of waste paper as a raw material. China, which imports around 26 million tons of waste paper annually, is expected to use 6 million tons more as it steps up recycling. The US and Europe are also encouraging paper manufacturers to increase recycled content in paper.

India uses about 9 million tons of paper annually but only about 10% of that is recycled, because of the absence of organized collection systems and low awareness of segregating waste at source. When paper waste mixes with other organic waste it cannot be used for recycling and is truly 'wasted', industry experts said. India now imports close to 5 million tons of waste paper to produce a range of products.

ITC Sonar First Hotel to Earn Carbon Credits

ITC Hotels has set a precedence by possibly becoming the first hospitality chain in the world to have earned carbon credits. Its luxury property, ITC Sonar in Kolkata, which switched to energy-efficient CFL bulbs as part of its energy-saving drive, has been issued 1,996 carbon credits per annum for a period of 10 years. The project has been registered as a clean development mechanism project (CDM) at the United Nations (UNFCCC).

The carbon credits earned by the hotel through its energy efficiency process can be capitalized to add to its revenues. One carbon credit is equivalent to reduction of one ton of carbon dioxide. Carbon credits are currently trading at around euro 12 per unit. However, ITC has no immediate plans to sell its carbon credits as the price is currently low. The hotel had applied to the CDM executive board with total reductions of 2,987 metric tons of carbon dioxide per annum. However, the hotel qualified to earn 1,996 carbon credits per annum. India's second largest hospitality chain brought on board international consultancy firm Price water house-Coopers (PwC) to measure its carbon footprint and ITC Sonar, which was unveiled in 2002, was selected as a pilot project. The 238-room hotel has been using energy-conserving CFL bulbs and energy-efficient air conditioning appliances, solar water heating equipment, and improved pumping systems, among other such initiatives. 'The journey to reduce greenhouse gas emissions is going on. The same will be reflected at all ITC properties,' said Tarun Chattopadhyay, chief engineer of ITC Sonar. 'ITC Sonar is the first hotel in the world to have earned carbon credits,' he said. PwC is also in the process of mapping carbon footprint at ITC's other properties. ITC Hotels operates the ITC Luxury Collection, ITC Sheraton.

Globally, even though other hotels such as Four Seasons, Mandarin Oriental, Ritz-Carlton, Taj, and Leela have been implementing eco-friendly measures, ITC is probably the first to earn carbon credits. Some like Starwood have even launched green hotels called 'Element'. The CDM fund expected from the project activity is expected to encourage Indian hotels for investing in energy-efficient initiative which would contribute towards meeting the energy demand of the country at large

Conclusions

The ITC has focused on various Marketing strategies according to which they have made in their marketing strategies, these are:

A) Sourcing Capability—ITC has strong sourcing capabilities. With the help of various sources, ITC was able to extend its business in different sectors.
They entered into FMCG after establishing a strong base in the agricultural sector.

The wheat from the agricultural sector held in establishing a market for the Aashirvaad atta. Similarly, ITC used its various sources very effectively and efficiently.

B) Effective Brand Utilization—After getting recognized in the agricultural and FMCG sector, ITC used its established brand name for entering into the stationary market.

They introduced Classmate by ITC which helped them in grabbing a good market share.

Know how to do effective Business Branding.

C) Related Businesses—ITC had very interrelated businesses. This helped them in the in-house production of their raw materials.

For example, ITC used its paperboard business for the packaging of its various products. It reduced the costs and need for outsourcing.

D) Role of Management—Management is the heart and soul of a successful business. Having a leader like YC Deveshwar helped ITC in reaching heights.

E) Focus on Sustainability—ITC focuses on sustainability as its goal. Major projects of ITC are focusing on Sustainability.

They have targeted majorly those sectors which are sustainable in the long run, offering more growth.

F) Meeting CSR—ITC focuses on fulfilling its social responsibility. This aspect is very important in today's scenario.

They started serving the society in Sarapaka, an economically backward area in Andhra Pradesh. ITC contributed to the development of education, environmental protection, and community development.

Case Questions

1. How do you assess the business strategy and corporate social responsibility policy of ITC—Are they completely in sync or ITC has sacrificed many business growth opportunities due to its tag of manufacturing so-called sin products like cigarettes.

2. Why is ITC (Indian Tobacco Company) not changing its brand name from ITC to any other name which will detach its association with tobacco products?

2

The Enlightened 'Employee Unions'

A Case Study of Negotiating with Knowledge Workers and their Unions

Learning Objectives

To identify the advent of Internet Technology and the globalized markets. To discuss about the commitment to cost, quality, and time, that have been the most essential factors to ensure business survival. To understand their roles and responsibilities, correctly and effectively towards a common objective of continuing to be in business. To identify the IT implosion in all aspects of business management. To find a paradigm shift in the approach to negotiations between the employer and the employees. To discuss about the current state of peaceful and productive employee relations (ER).

Synopsis

The IT implosion in all aspects of business management also has demanded appropriate levels of education and training in the skills required at all levels of an organization. Today everyone from the gate security to the salesmen is required to be computer literate to be able to manage their day-to-day organizational roles. Every workman (sorry, they need to be addressed as 'Associates') in today's situation needs to be able to handle operations which are in majority of cases computer-controlled. In general this has led to an overall improvement of the educational levels at all

Indian Business Case Studies. Sandeep Pachpande, Asha Pachpande, and J A Kulkarni, Oxford University Press.
© ASM Group of Institutes, Pune, India 2022. DOI: 10.1093/oso/9780192869371.003.0002

business processes and also in understanding, the parameters which decide the business survival.

The Case Contents

The employee unions and their leaders are no exception to this trend. Over a period of the previous one decade we normally do not hear of violent labour disturbances and slogan mongering and red flag demonstrations in the major industrial estates across India. There appears to be a sea change in the attitude and approach to employee-related negotiations which are done across the table or on a continuous basis between the affected parties, using all modern methods of communications such as presentations, deliberations involving members of the parties to the negotiations on equal footing, trying to understand each other's viewpoints more constructively and in the long-term interests of organization.

This case study attempts to focus on the above and look for sustainability issues of this paradigm change and seeks the participants valued comments on the perpetuity of the current state of peaceful and productive employee relations (ER).

Few examples of educated unionism:

1. The garment and allied workers union gawu (Garment and Allied Workers Union):

This union covers a recognized employee union of the garment workers largely from Gurgaon-Manesar-Bhiwandi belt. One of the major units in this belt is the VIVA Global the main supplier of readymade garments from Marks & Spencer's.

The major issue related to the working conditions for the labour force in the manufacturing setup is due to extremely hot ambient temperatures and lack of drinking water facilities. What is important to be noted is that the union leader of GAWU is Mrs Ananya Bhattacharjee, who is a computer science degree holder from the Texas University and has worked in global software giants in the Silicon Valley in the US. Mrs Ananya Bhattacharjee (a lady in her fifties) is driven by her conviction that she needs to resolve the problems faced by the workmen due to high handedness of the respective management. She believed that in order to achieve her deeper intentions of fighting against injustice on the downtrodden that, she has to be with the society where such exploitations happen.

Mrs Ananya was able to pick up all the serious issues of the Garment workers at VIVA Global, and through her concerted efforts and extensive use of internet-based communications, was able to get VIVA black listed from the buyers' community but also got the global attention drawn towards the plight of the workers through effective internet campaigning and collective bargaining. VIVA management while rectifying the maladies of the workmen realized the writing on the wall that they need to be proactive in resolving issues of the workmen and treat them their feelings with due respect and empathy. On a similar footing Mrs Ananya also got the issues at the Walmart operations to get the equivalent floor level wages for its employees in its Indian operations.

Today GAWU has nearly 3000 workmen as its members. Today the industrial belt has lots of harmony and positively oriented Industrial Relations (IR) climate. All this has been possible due to the professional approach inculcated by the union leader in most of the units and making the managements conscious of their responsibilities

2. Maruti Suzuki employees union:

Most of us are aware of the recent labour unrest in the Manesar plants of MSUL. But what is seen as an eye-opener is that the workers union is exhibiting leadership and organizational skills of higher degree rather than slogan mongering or violent protests or militancy.

One more thing which is highly perceptible is the coming together and working together of nearly 11 unions in the area and conducting meetings to reengineer their tactics to rally the total unorganized sector and voice their demands on a common platform. In the common meetings of union leaders they even discuss issues such as general price rise due to inflation, various disinvestment strategies adopted by scrupulous managements, and other industry-specific issues from long-term points of interests for the members of the unions.

One more important aspect which needs to be noted is that these union leaders would not like to involve any political leader in their efforts to get their issues resolved. They express the feeling that 'Politics without dynamic grass roots experience is a corrupt politicization of Labor issues'.

3. Honda motorcycles and scooters India (HMSI): The union at HMSI is led by an internal union which proudly claims that they have been

able to weed out all the past misunderstandings and now they involve themselves in resolving even the issues faced by the management in the smooth running of the operations.

A glaring example of such an initiative by the union at HMSI to help the management in resolving the managements issue was its participation in the meeting with the vendors of the company in making them agree to shift their base of operations from Haryana to Rajasthan, where HMSI is to establish a new factory which the vendors were refusing with the management reps.

4. Toyota Kirloskar employees union: The employee union at the Toyota Kirloskar plant near Bengaluru in Karnataka recently introduced a new productivity increase proposal by the management. On the same issue there was likely to be a violent strike by the union, since they felt that the management was using pressure tactics and keeping the union in dark about the process to be followed for achieving the targeted productivity increase.

But wiser counsels prevailing the management decided to make a detailed presentation to the union on the issue of productivity increase and allowed the union to testify the new process through seeking professional guidance from outside. This resulted in an amicable settlement between the management and the union.

The union leader said: 'Earlier the management's stance was hostile and it did not want to discuss anything with the workers, but they realized that the strikes are self defeating and cause loss of production. Now members of the management team even agree to correct their mistakes during negotiations.'

Mr Tapansen, MP and general secretary of CITU says, 'In 90%companies today, the workers want increase in productivity, because they get better incentives that way'. This indicates a marked difference and departure from tester years when the workers vehemently opposed any move by the management to demand increased productivity.

It is a common scene now a day that during productivity and wage negotiations the union leaders extensively use laptops and presentations. And substantiate their stand by providing global data on compensations versus productivity. It is also seen that in quite few cases there are MBA degree holders amongst the union representatives

In fact recently a delegation from German union leaders visited to study the strategy followed by unions in Indian operations which enable smooth negotiations between the management and the workers union without any strikes or violence.

The case of UNITES, a Bangalore based union representing the IT/ITES employees, led by the union leader who was till recently a team leader in a call centre job, with nearly 18000 members from 500 companies, is the largest readdress body for IT employees in India. The union regularly conducts web-based campaigns, emails, and over social media including Facebook and Twitter. The union committee meets every two months locally and once a year nationally. The union has successfully thwarted attempts by few foreign companies shift their base from India to other locations resulting in mass retrenchment and prevailed on the managements to reverse their decisions.

It appears from the international labour union scenario that they have delinked from any political affiliations. In the UK and US, there are powerful unions negotiating with individual employers without any political clout. The same is seen across European countries and even in Japan. The role of the unions has become more focused on negotiations with the employers rather than dealing through political contacts.

The Outcome

Due to professional approach of Ms Ananya, serious issues running into the manufacturing belt was raised on digital platforms. Due to professional approach inculcated by the union leader in most of the units and making the managements conscious of their responsibilities.

Highly educated union leaders proved excellent style of leadership and organization skills helped in resolving various issues on a common platform, and resolving the issues without any political leader's involvement. They express the feeling that 'Politics without dynamic grass roots experience is a corrupt politicization of Labor issues'.

The tactics of involving the operations and management to resolve managerial issues and misunderstandings helped in smooth running of production and operations.

Emerging technologies have brought a drastic change to solve disputes between the management and the workers union without any strikes and violence. With the help of presentations management was able to explain the cause of loss of productivity.

Future Scenario

Educated union leaders would help in the increase of future production. Educated union leaders would play a major role in resolving employee disputes and negotiations.

Technology and social platforms would be the latest trend to voice out internal issues, which may lead into the defaming activity of the organization. Tech-savvy leaders can be the best strategies in understanding the market trends, economic situations, and national and international business environment.

Conclusion

The union has successfully thwarted attempts by few foreign companies shift their base from India to other locations resulting in mass retrenchment and prevailed on the managements to reverse their such decisions.

It appears from the international labour union scenario that they have delinked from any political affiliations. In the UK and US, there are powerful unions negotiating with individual employers without any political clout. The same is seen across European countries and even in Japan. The role of the unions has become more focused on negotiations with the employers rather than dealing through political contacts.

Case Questions

1. Do you think the scenario as explained in the above case is a reality and is there to stay hereafter for major industrial estates across the country?

2. What strategy do you suggest could be adopted by major industry blocks in the country to establish a very long-term peaceful IR in spite of volatile market and economic situations at the national and international business environments.

3. With the Individual Union Leaders having expertise in the business processes the role of government in IR management seems to be becoming irrelevant, do you think it is good for the unions and the employers in the long term?

3

The Triumphant 'Trikaya Coating Pvt Ltd'

A Case Study of an Addicted Entrepreneur

Learning Objectives

How does an entrepreneurial idea motivate someone to instinctively jump on to every available way out to materialize an enterprise to start and establish. This case also highlights mostly common and few uncommon issues which the entrepreneur has to face and follow an attitude of never say die. What is the real pleasure in seeing your own small firm flourish in to a successful business set up as envy of many of your competitors.

Case Details

Mr Ram Jorapurkar was trying to relax in his armchair in his new spacious residence at a serene location in the city of Nasik in Maharashtra. His restless mind was busy chewing the remotest and latest happenings in his personal and business life reminding him of the successful and not so pleasant incidences of his climb to the present state of affairs.

Ram Jorapurkar, belongs to a highly orthodox and traditional family background. Born and brought up in Mumbai, the hectic lifestyle however had its influence on right from his school age. His mind even then was busy trying for an alternate way of life compared to the regimental environment at home and the surroundings. While maintaining the

Indian Business Case Studies. Sandeep Pachpande, Asha Pachpande, and J A Kulkarni, Oxford University Press.
© ASM Group of Institutes, Pune, India 2022. DOI: 10.1093/oso/9780192869371.003.0003

decorum at home Ram started looking for breaking out from the shackles of conventional schooling and higher studies, definitely not inclined to study for a 9 to 5 p.m. job/career in a government office or industry as an employee.

At an early age of 17 to 20 years he expressed his attitude towards doing something unique unconventional and dare devilish in a dire contrast to the expectations of the family. At 20 years he had developed his friend's circle and acquaintances with some political big wigs who understanding his revolutionary approach provided him with the necessary outlet to his frustrations of not being able to tread the family dictum. For Ram being able to earn a regular salary through a job was never of any fulfilment or career he always looked for entrepreneurial opportunities even before he completed his studies. But for his parents this was an unacceptable behavioural or growth norm, they expressed their dislike to Ram and sometimes through family friends urging him to amend his approach to life and follow the time-tested way of settling in a job as a career and getting married and following the family traditions as adapted by his elder brothers.

It was some time in the 1980s that Ram decided that enough was enough and decided to quit the family ambience and took up a part-time job as a stepping stone for his future objectives of being his own employer. While working in the job in a paint manufacturing firm in western suburbs of Mumbai, Ram strengthened his links with the political contacts to leverage resources for plunging in to an entrepreneurial venture. However the lack of formal education and training in the technical aspects of any product or process technology hindered his aspirations to latch on to a firm business idea. For some time he took up marketing activity of his employer products to familiarize himself with how people in business behave and interact on professional matters, wanting to learn by himself the way in which procurement and selling functions are handled in business. Simultaneously Ram tried to look for opportunities to engage himself in the businesses of the customers to his present organization then.

In around 1990 or so Ram decided to step out of his regular employment and start catering to the sundry requirements of paints and its derivatives as a small agent to stock and sell the products himself. Ram had borrowed a two-wheeler from his friend on rental basis to meet his travel requirements for his selling agency and had hired some small go down to stock his daily and weekly requirements for sale. During his nearly 4–5 years of hard work as a selling agent for industrial and domestic requirements paints and chemicals, Ram could tie up with few of his friends who were interested in developing some engineering sheet metal components and related surface coating to the customers of paints in furniture and auto ancillaries industries. This called for some investments and partnering with some small-scale units in western suburbs. Ram leveraged his contacts and industry friends for necessary help in acquiring necessary seed capital and borrowing limits from banks to meet his investments and working capital needs.

However his earnings were not sufficient to allow him to settle down for some time but his family members continued although from distance that for the sake of family prestige at least he should get back to settled way of regular earnings, this became more intense since his father also retired from his regular daily work and his elder brothers had stable jobs and had got married and took care of his parents. There was also a pressure from his elders to get him married and settle down as in case of his brothers. However Ram was convinced that his efforts of establishing an independent business would result in success all he needed was some more perseverance and hard work for which he was ready to face any amount of hard work and sleepless nights. By the year 2000 Ram was able to breathe little safely and had developed his business with seemingly assuring savings and decided to settle himself on the family front and got married and started staying in an owned apartment in Mumbai. Unfortunately he lost his beloved father around this time (it was Ram's father who while expressing anxiety at times was discretely supportive and believed in Ram's capabilities as an entrepreneur).

Ram as per his basic instinct was satisfied with the progress he had made in his business and felt that he needed to move out of Mumbai to look for opportunities to grow his business. It was around this time Ram decided to explore market opportunities in the neighbouring city of Nasik. Ram carried out an informal market survey of likely customers to his business of sheet metals and surface coating. He could go through some leads and contacts in industries at Nasik. For few initial years Ram used to do up and down trips to Nasik, irrespective of his personal and family concerns he continued to exert himself to the maximum till such time he was convinced that Nasik industries offered him better and long-term business prospects compared to his efforts in Mumbai based customers. It was in 2003–2004 Ram decided to spend more time in Nasik and started staying in Nasik in rented house and reduced his frequency of travel to Mumbai but due to schooling and other difficulties he maintained his family in Mumbai.

All said and done the constant rush of business-related activities, negligence towards timely and proper food and family matters Ram suffered loneliness and he was losing his otherwise robust health. As destiny had in his bad luck during his far of stay in Nasik two of his beloved children the eldest daughter and youngest son were victims of cancer at an early age of ten and six respectively. This was a near fatal and body blow to Ram and his wife who had at times lost complete hope of stability and happiness in their family life and were totally distraught and shattered in their confidence level. There was no one to work as an anchor to their lives and no place to find any solace. For quite a few months Ram decided to stay put in Mumbai to provide some company and support to his wife and the only daughter Tejashwini who gave them some comfort as a child (she is now grown to be a promising youngster doing her Engineering studies at Nasik).

After the initial turbulence the never say quits nature of Ram pulled him back to the business he had just initiated in Nasik. Perhaps Ram started engaging himself more rigorously in his enterprise in order to get out of the deep depression he and his family members had undergone.

Ram finally executed all the initial investments and organizational details for his maiden venture and named the enterprises by the omnipresent meaning as 'Trikaya Industries'. The location was an ideal one since it was amidst all major industries in the Satpur Industrial Estate of Nasik with its main customer the M&M Ltd Nasik being very much in the vicinity. The uniqueness in the establishment was so evident that it surpassed all the sacrifices and challenges a human being could face in oneself and without any sort of support from any one nearer to him. He was determined to test his capabilities come what may at times being called as heartless human. During this time he toiled hard with the determination of the Phoenix.

About Trikaya Industries

Renamed as Trikaya Coatings Pvt Ltd started in an area of nearly 75,000 sqft enough to accommodate the installation of all essential equipment for handling of sheet metal bodies (load carriers) of SUVs and related items, degreasing and surface coating units for such jobs, necessary requirements for sheet metal component repairs including welding sets and cleaning and deburring operations.

The capacity installed to meet the batch type surface coating of load bodies of M&M jeeps (for Bolero and Armada versions to start with, the unit had to keep in pace with varied requirements of its major customer the M&M Ltd and its strategic sourcing plans).

Trikaya, understanding the manufacturing strategies of its major customers, had to expand/diversify vertically to be able to effectively take up manufacture and surface coating of huge structures like cargo bodies for M&M Ltd. This called for fresh investments in high-capacity high-speed presses and also identify with the help of its own customers the procurement of sheet metal and connected toolings required for the complete manufacture of load bodies for the cargo vehicles of M&M. This called for real 'guts' to risk investments based on only one major customer like M&M. M&M Ltd also true to its principles of professional practices provided all the necessary help and guidance to Trikaya for its vertical growth in terms supply of complete carriers ready for final assembly on to the vehicles.

The above while straining the business and in particular the financial limitations of Trikaya offered the toughest journey so far the entrepreneurial guts of Ram Jorapurkar. It is worth noting that Ram was carrying out all his responsibilities effectively in spite of staying alone in Nasik and only when the time permitted or combined with business needs could visit his family in Mumbai.

The installed capacity by 2012–2013 has grown up to several sheet metal presses of capacity varying between 75 T and 315 T at the rate of 16,000 strokes per day on a 12 hour shift basis (i.e., 110 load bodies manufacture per day). The overall investment in plant and machinery is around Rs 1.50 Crores as on date). Trikaya adopts both batch types for sheet metal and continuous process for surface coating operations.

As regards to process quality, the standards required and managed by Trikaya are around Cpk> 1.33 and are driven by its Original Equipment (OE) customers and process rejections below of less than 0.50 %. In order to achieve better utilization and operating margins the unit has to operate around 85% capacity utilization. The organizational structure is more centralized and Ram and his immediate team are empowered to take all daily and operations decisions.

The present operative strength of personnel employed including Ram is 60 workmen and 25 supervisory and staff functions. Ram with his down to earth management style and having himself grown up from the ranks has effectively managed the overall morale of his employees. This is vindicated by non-existence of any labour union at Trikaya and everyone at the operative level rising to the challenges time and again to enable successful implementation of growth and diversification plans. Ram is highly proactive in not only with his customer requirements, is also constantly tuned in to the minute issues at the factory. He has set in himself as a role model of untiring efforts in spite of major issues and singularly focused on his Trikaya of which he can never get detached even for rest and relaxation.

The present issues in production process are maintaining rework requirements to minimum which call for appropriate investment in terms of tool reconditioning facility, to reduce time spent in deburring and other rework. Especially with its customers demanding ready to assemble parts and subassemblies it would absolutely necessary for Trikaya to be ready with improved processes, may have introduced Robotic Weld lines for accuracy and assured quality as manufactured.

The existing competition even though manageable could offer tough competition as the market for auto industry tags on to growth in its marketplace and fresh investments by OE and few major competitors. Trikaya also has to keep a close watch on product substitutions which might adversely affect its current lines of manufacture. The major competition is from Mungi Bros Pvt Ltd and Panse Auto Pvt Ltd for stampings including auto ancillary major JBM, MUSCO & Reliable Tech Pvt Ltd.

Trikaya is a direct supplier to its OE customers and does not so far have any agencies for distribution marketing. For that matter it is 100% dependent on the business plans of its OE customers. It has so far met its finance requirements for capital equipment partly from its own resources and partly as loans from banks. Its working capital requirements are served through bank finance which responds meticulously by scheduled repayments.

The major suppliers to Trikaya are Bhushan Steel Ltd, Sana Steel Ltd and have around 26 sub-vendors for subassemblies and finished parts for cargo body.

Future Plans of Trikaya

Immediate growth plans include catering to NMC cargo manufacture and look for opportunities in the railway coach components such as seats and toilets components in view of 100% FDI policy announced by GOI. Trikaya also has plans to explore the export potential for its process and supply capabilities of OE customers abroad. While aiming at these future plans Trikaya is aware of the global standards productivity and quality standards of its operations (working towards zero defect level) and implementation of TS16949, lean manufacturing, TQM, 5S and other quality and productivity global standards and 100% schedule adherence.

Trikaya aspires to be in the row of Rs.100 crore turnover companies by 2018 with 15 to 20% profit (EBITDA) margins. The larger focus would be to improve its financial leverage for future investments along with organizational restructuring for strategic business approach and to broad base its training and development of its personnel for present and future business plans. Better cash flow management is a highly essential aspect on which it needs to work relentlessly. Trikaya has got nearly 40 to 50,000 sqft of land available for its future expansion and diversification plans.

Trikaya at Crossroads

Even though Trikaya is almost three decades old, the top management is constantly worried about the strategic product and process changes at its OE customers since its entire business is dependent on the continuity of OE business and the respective growth plans of its competition. Trikaya has grown to a level of operations (threshold limits) that any major change in the auto industry would be directly influencing its business prospects.

Not having an independent product of its own is one of the major risks Trikaya carries over its prospects. The new product while ensuring utilization of existing capabilities has to be in line with the current process technologies available at Trikaya as would also be only marginally stretching its skill levels of its operative personnel. Even though raising project finance may be not a very difficult task but it has to avoid playing itself into the hands of unscrupulous VC funds. Besides it is handicapped by lack of the basic strengths of project planning function in terms of a comprehensive approach and long-term perspectives of assured business growth in future.

In terms of finance, technology, and people strengths Trikaya has been successful so far but does not express adequate confidence for achieving its future strategic plans. Besides the partners and rest are so much used to present levels and lines of business that any future project would almost need a paradigm shift in its capability to draw itself gradually out of the clutches of job work to manufacturing product of its own. This what is on the top of mind for Ram Jorapurkar, the addicted entrepreneur who perhaps has so far put in the best of his capability and efforts and looks forward to pragmatic and feasible growth plan for his creation of the Trikaya.

Conclusions

The case study is a typical model for all aspiring entrepreneurs and students of entrepreneurship as a course of studies as to how in uncertain circumstances what really helps is the gut feel of the entrepreneur and the commitment and conviction he brings to his enterprise in spite of teardown stress and hurdles.

Case Questions

1. Do you feel that the entrepreneur in Ram Jorapurkar has come to a threshold limit in terms of his entrepreneurial scope and long-term stability?

2. What would you decide or would have decided differently some time ago in the business cycle of Trikaya to avoid the crossroads syndrome/situation?

3. What business or product project plan would you offer to Trikaya for long-terms prospects and perpetuation of its healthy growth so far?

.

4

Building an Ethical and Smart Organization

Learning Objectives

All businesses are complex organizational systems that are nested within larger systems, such as national cultures and legal and regulatory systems, and composed of individuals who bring their own values and perspectives to work.

This interplay of personal, organizational, and regulatory systems creates a dynamic environment that must be actively managed by leaders to promote the company's long-term success. Ethical failure at any level can bring catastrophe, but achieving good ethics at all levels yields enormous benefits in trust, efficiency, and happiness.

Synopsis

In difficult financial times, companies face various moral issues to try to keep up with their competitors. Although these issues have a direct impact on employee decision making, businesses rarely address how employees should assess the ethics of their actions and incorporate ethics into their decisions. Often this can be alleviated by creating and maintaining a corporate culture with a focus on ethics. Corporate culture is often considered to be both a source of various problems and the basis for solutions and is certainly a factor that determines how people behave in an organization. The role of management in the organizational culture is important as it both acts as a role model for the employees and

Indian Business Case Studies. Sandeep Pachpande, Asha Pachpande, and J A Kulkarni, Oxford University Press.
© ASM Group of Institutes, Pune, India 2022. DOI: 10.1093/oso/9780192869371.003.0004

can also directly influence the behaviour and culture to improve organizational performance. Of course there are better methods that management can use to incorporate ethics into the corporate culture or increase the likelihood that its employees will act ethically and these methods are explored.

Introduction

When one evaluates the reasons for the fall of companies such as Enron, Lehman Brothers, and WorldCom, what connects the dots is a stupefying disregard for ethics. Closer home, Ranbaxy's recent run-in with the US Food and Drug Administration has invited renewed questions about the governance, compliance, and ethics practices of a section of firms in India and indeed across global economies.

While there is no reassurance in stating that incidents like Ranbaxy or Wockhardt or the fact that some of India's best-selling small cars have failed independent crash tests conducted by a global car safety watchdog are aberrations rather than reflections of a systemic problem, misconduct within its own walls remains one of the most lethal threats to any organization. Put in another way, a lack of ethics is like a missed opportunity in a world where competitive advantage is fast becoming a commodity. Says Rita McGrath, a professor at Columbia Business School, and author of the End of Competitive Advantage, 'Companies can build advantages on the basis of ethics. High ethical standards tend to be correlated with other positive attributes such as attention to quality, fair dealings with people and transparency that can give organizations an advantage'. Needless to say, the benefits of good corporate governance and a culture of ethics percolate down to all levels of stakeholders—investors and top-quality employees are attracted to ethical companies.

Given that, what are the challenges that prevent companies from embracing and—more importantly—sustaining a culture of ethics and good conduct? What are the ways in which companies can ensure they don't stray from their intent at the time of establishment? And what is the best way to react if a situation involving an ethical transgression does arise?

Ethical Corporate Culture

In his book the Tipping Point, Malcolm Gladwell has spoken about the 'Broken Windows' theory that draws from the field of criminology. It states that crime tends to increase in situations where the atmosphere reflects that 'anything goes'. If a broken window is not repaired, it somehow gives a message that it is okay to break more windows. The norm applies in the corporate setting too.

Integrity, which is one of the core values of any organization, should be held above all other forms of behaviour. 'At the heart of an ethical culture are the shared values and assumptions of the people in the organization. These provide the overall direction for the behavior of employees,' says Mona Cheriyan, director, Human Resources, ASK Group.

'A strict enforcement of codes of compliance and a culture of zero intolerance for malpractices and frauds deter any probable ethical lapses,' adds Abhay Gupte, senior director, Deloitte.

Having said that, it is difficult for a company to decide and craft an ethical corporate culture somewhere down its journey. It has to be done right at the beginning. 'It should be in the DNA of the promoters and leaders, and must be part of everything that the company does from day one,' says Narayan PS, Vice President and Head, sustainability, Wipro.

While we know that senior leaders set the tone for action, they do not by themselves achieve the outcome for the organization. It is how leaders act to promote right action that determines the performance and the culture. 'While ethical codes may vary from company to company, the basic fabric remains the same,' says Dilep Misra, president and head, Corporate Human Resources, JK Tier.

At all times, management must take cognizance of staff turnover and grievances, customer complaints, product defects, and returned items, expressed dissatisfaction of contractors and suppliers, cases of litigation triggered by unethical behaviour, and community unhappiness with corporate behaviour as reflected by media reports, citizen protests, etc. 'The prevailing environment in society is so poor and corruption is so widespread, that creating an oasis of ethics is challenging. The only way out is that the tone has to be set at the top, else ethics will just be lip service,' says Ravi Venkatesan, author and former chairman, Microsoft India.

Ethics also includes placing the organization's interest before the promoter's interest. 'For instance, the employment of a promoter's son should be driven on merit and not on anything else,' says Harish Mariwala, chairman and MD, Marico.

Often those integrity failures are a result of senior individuals crossing ethical boundaries. 'In a hurry to reach to the top and to beat competition, they compromise on ethics,' says author and leadership guru Ms Rao. One must note that having a culture of ethics and compliance in a corporation is not a guarantee that there will not be breaches. What saves a company is the swiftness with which it redresses its wound.

Formal Elements of Ethical Culture

The Tata Group, known for its high 'trust' quotient, believes creating an ethical culture is a journey 'from compliance to commitment to consciousness'. 'It is not a question of the number of rules, but embedding desired values in each employee's consciousness, so that ethical conduct is a spontaneous output,' says Mukund Rajan, member, group executive council, and chief ethics officer, Tata Sons.

To make core values explicit, and to demonstrate how they translate into behaviour in the daily business, an organization should establish formal norms, including codes of conduct, and guidelines and these should be led from the top, says Cheriyan of ASK Group.

Some prerequisites can help a corporation foster ethics in its DNA: there should be clearly enunciated policies, abasic code of conduct, regular communication with employees, and a swift investigation system in case of reported malpractices. Here the perspective and role of corporate boards of directors in overseeing ethics and compliance matters within their firms cannot be underestimated.

The Board could also insist on a compliance certificate every quarter, and this certificate ought to be vetted by the audit committee. In fact, audits are good detection mechanisms to keep a tight leash on transgressions—a type of consequence management. In simple words, audits form the execution part of an ethical culture. While internal audits help create a culture of ethics, external audits give out a message to outsiders about the internal culture of ethics. 'The Board must mete out punishment, including sacking the CEO if he is found guilty,' says TV Mohandas Pai, chairman, Manipal.

Global Education Services, and an ex-Infosys hand. 'Once the punishment is certain, the culture is firmed up.' That is the easier part, the benefits of which have been well documented. What is critical is to understand that ethics is different from compliance. The latter is the straightforward 'rules and regulations' part of ethics, and doesn't require high education. Ethics is a larger universe that goes beyond just following the law, and therefore, reflects how a company is oriented. It is possible for a company to be legally compliant and yet not have a strong culture of ethics.

The process of creating a culture of ethics probably starts from the process of recruitment. While hiring a person, it is not enough to assess only his/her professional and technical competencies. It is equally important to look at the fit with the values of integrity and ethics. Here's how Wipro does it: its employees—campus and lateral hires—are inducted into Wipro's ethics journey at the very start of their association with the company. Thereafter, mandatory annual test and certification process, leadership training sessions, electronic mailers, posters, etc. constantly guide employees to follow the Wipro Code of Business Conduct (COBC). Any breach of COBC, identified from concerns raised through Wipro's Ombuds process, is handled swiftly and with seriousness, reveals Padmanabhan A, similar plane, the Board at JK Corporation meets every quarter to check on compliance breaches.

Challenges for Sustaining an Ethical Culture

But sustaining an ethical culture doesn't come without its challenges. It is particularly difficult to create and sustain this culture in a dispersed global organization. First, you have to define the culture and create a shared meaning of ethics across the organization. For instance, a media house may prohibit giving or receiving gifts, which could be an ethical guideline. But in India, gifting is accepted as part of culture, so a guideline like that could go against the popular wisdom, which poses a challenge.

Second, how do you propagate the non-negotiable? 'If you define many things under ethics, the education challenge in the company is high,' says Santrupt Misra, CEO, Carbon Black Business and group HR director,

Aditya Birla Group. But the real moment of truth is how a company re-acts to the ethical crisis. Does it wait for someone to point it out or accept it publicly and make corrections proactively? Or worse—does it play the blame game? That apart, ambitious Indian company wanting to play the global field must bear in mind that often, norms of the West may be more stringent than the ones back home. Critical lapses may not be overlooked so easily, as the case of Ranbaxy demonstrates. This is also a shift from the experiences of the past, when expectations from Indian companies were low. 'It is now important for corporate India to match up to global stand-ards,' says Mariwala.

A handful of companies the strategist spoke to argued if they were to comply with all the innumerable laws, it will slow processes down. 'But in the long run, look at the damage you will do to your own reputation and brand salience if you don't comply. You will have a longer ground to cover,' says Rajeev Dubey, president, group HR, corporate services and aftermarket, Mahindra & Mahindra. 'At the end of the day, good reputa-tion means good business. And reputation can't be outsourced.'

SMART Ranbaxy's recent run-in with the US Food and Drug Administration has invited renewed questions about how to strengthen compliance mechanisms and ethical leadership within firms.

Conclusions

Ethical issues have posed major challenges to companies in recent years and there will undoubtedly be more in the future. Good ethical practices may not be easy to maintain. However, with a well-designed ethics policy, ethical leadership and implementing ethics into organizational strategies and processes will make it easier. The reason is because these factors are incorporated into the organizational culture. How might a culture of character be developed? It is certainly by intention. It is the responsibility of particular individuals within the organization, that is, its leadership. Strong leaders model and pass on ethical aspects of the culture and use techniques like structure, decision-making processes, rewards, norms, heroes, stories, rituals, and other artefacts to create a strong culture. This is the foundation for creating a culture of character, where members of the organization 'know what is right, value what is right, and do what is right'.

In all cases, management must be committed to ethical conduct. To conclude, despite the economic crisis, there are clear and long-lasting advantages of establishing an ethical culture. With a more open and ethical organizational culture, the more positively employees tend to commit to corporate social responsibility and this will generate more honest environments. As a consequence, this may not only reduce the unhealthy environment that began the financial crisis, but will also help in restoring the health of the financial system that caused it

Case Questions

1. Are workers at all levels encouraged to take responsibility for the consequences of their behaviour? To question authority when they are asked to do something that they consider to be wrong? How?

2. What is your overall evaluation of the organizations ethical culture? What are its areas of strength and weakness?

3. Does a formal code of ethics and/or values exist? Is it distributed? How widely is it used? Is it reinforced in other formal systems, such as reward and decision-making systems?

5

The Directors and the In Directors

A Case Study in 'Corporate Governance'

Learning Objectives

To analyse the need for the concept of corporate governance. To assess the impact of globalization on business ethics. To evaluate the association between the degree of material comfort attained by mankind and the tendency to blatantly flout norms.

Synopsis

Over the previous few years we have been hearing about the issues in 'Corporate Governance' (CG) in the corporate circles and through the claims at the various industry associations such as the CII, ASSOCHAM, FICCI, and few others. To a common man who has a very superficial understanding about the happenings in Indian business scenario, this appears to be yet another jargon meant for the publicity purposes of the concerned business units to attract the attention of the commoner to indicate that they are up to incorporating some altogether new techniques of business management through which their superiority over the others in competition needs to be differentiated. But the 'Aamadmi' is not able to locate even a distant indication of any improvements at the marketplace due to these claims of CG and the 'bla–bla' that happens at the board meetings. For him the things have moved from bad to worse in the products and services he was used to so far. The big malls and multiplexes have taken away the personal contacts, credit terms and the affordable prices, and near home locations he was used to till recently.

Indian Business Case Studies. Sandeep Pachpande, Asha Pachpande, and J A Kulkarni, Oxford University Press.
© ASM Group of Institutes, Pune, India 2022. DOI: 10.1093/oso/9780192869371.003.0005

Corporate Governance: A Utopian Concept?

CG in India is a comparatively new concept (not necessarily new in its philosophy and ground rules). As a sequel to liberalization and globalization of the Indian economy, all the concerned were exposed to the global requirements of ethical and legal ways of conducting business internationally. Initially the government did appoint various committees of well-known business leaders such as the committee headed by Mr Rahul Bajaj, Mr Kumarmangalam Birla, Mr Narayan Murthy of Infosys. Subsequently, the company law board and SEBI have provided guidelines in the form of definite sections of the CLB & Listing Norms, etc. for evaluating and certifying the corporations' eligibility to carry out businesses in India and abroad. In case of mergers and acquisitions the competition committee looks into the compliance aspects to provide support and protections to the stakeholders in the business. Many organizations of course have adopted more stringent CG norms in their business practices to ensure compliance to the ethical and legally permissible operating practices in the conduct of their businesses. In order to ensure protection of the stakeholders interests, further rules have been made in the CG compliance norms, the important ones being the appointment of Independent Directors (IDs) on the Boards of every listed company to monitor and control the greedy and sometimes illegal interests of the promoters for short-term gains, disregarding the long-term interests of the business and its stakeholders. CLB also recommends institution of various committees at the board and CEO levels of the companies to keep a constant watch on the various business transactions of the organizations including the remunerations paid to the senior-level executives. The role of the IDs is made more specific and are held responsible for oversight in the major business decisions made by the organization on which they are appointed as IDs. The role of the IDs is considered as comparable to and sometimes exceeding that of the external auditors of the company. The details of the credentials of the IDs are to be disclosed in the annual meetings of the shareholders and the appointments are to be approved by the shareholders. There is also a requirement that the remunerations paid to each of the IDs be included in the annual statement of accounts along with a compliance report on the other norms of CG. This is one of the reasons that the annual reports of various companies have become thicker in the recent years. The CG norms are also supposed to reflect the CSR initiatives of the organizations towards the society in which they operate as responsibilities towards its stakeholders. The annual reports also dwell in details about the various CSR projects undertaken by the companies. It is however to be noted that CSR activities of the major Indian Corporations such as the Tatas, Bajaj, and Birlas were more pronounced much before the CG initiatives in the globalized Indian business. In fact, there appears to be a lull in such initiatives post-globalization due to CG compliance requirements which perhaps have put certain constraints on the free-will initiatives towards CSR of these setups.

Does Spelling Out CG Norms Necessarily Build Trust?

CG even for the educated class appears like yet another exercise in vain like the ISO 9000, BS 9000 certification norms which had only very short-term impact in the last decade. As on today no one seems to bother about these norms of product and service quality amidst the rush of the 'Buy one get two free' labels which multiply the quality and performance issues (problems) of the same brand products of which the customers were more satisfied in their original 'Sons Ltd & Bros Ltd' shops and services. Popular brands such as Bajaj, Tata, Mafatlal, Park Avenue, Brook Bond, Colgate, etc., never needed in the past any such false incentives for promoting product sales and services at the markets. But as on today we are not sure if the same can be said about these very and other new players in spite of their compliance to the famous ISO, BS certificates and now with a new cap of compliance to the CG norms. The basic trust in the consistent quality and service standards seems to have been vitiated amidst claims of globalization and world-class standards. Even the respective company managements and the members of their boards often do not seem to agree with the correct interpretation and understanding of what good CG implies. In the most simple terminology 'Corporate Governance' refers to the commitment of the organization to carry out its normal and regular business, in the appropriate, legal, ethical, and transparent manner. Many however are confused in the correlation of this simple definition, and use the provisions of the guidelines to attract investors, and customers by producing volumes of write-ups in the company balance sheets, in the most glamorous words and styles of presentation towards compliance to CG norms. In fact it is a misnomer to term these as norms since there are no legally binding, effective, and evaluative norms on CG. Even at the global level there are more loopholes in the CG norms than the norms themselves. The recent episodes of Lehman Brothers, Enron, Goldman Sachs, not to forget Satyam of the Indian fame, the spicy events of the IPL, and the yet to unwind CWG are glaring instances of the loopholes being much wider and bigger than the provisions of CG and any other national or international legal and ethical norms of business. While teaching the topics on business ethics and morale, the concerned faculty necessarily quote the high sounding and glamorized 'Vision, Mission and Objectives' statements of major organizations in India and abroad to the students in management studies. Every faculty nowadays faces embarrassing situations, since the same companies are frequently caught on the wrong side of law of which once they had referred to as ideal or model examples of great organizations, noted for their commitment to ethical and legally transparent ways of conducting business. It becomes necessary for the faculty to give unbelievable excuses to ward off such distortions in the business-related behaviours of reputed companies to try to remove doubts and confusions in the minds of young students. As on today there will be more case studies on business failures due to the scandals rather than any sustainable success stories.

Reality Bites

The issue in this case is basically questioning the impact of compliance requirements of the CG and similar initiatives of the globalized economies. The instances of extreme contrasts between on paper claims of renowned companies. If we take a single example of Satyam Computers, we find that the Satyam Management was adjudged as the Indian company which has acquired global glory, mainly on account of its fair and highly ethical ways of doing business along with its major contribution in the form of major CSR initiatives.

There were expert committees to evaluate Satyam for such national and international level awards. All these committees were required to physically verify the status of compliance of CG and CSR initiatives at Satyam before bestowing the laurels. Within 24 hours after the chief architect of Satyam Mr Ramlingam Raju on the 7 January 2009 announced about the financial irregularities in Satyam, the entire world cried foul and declared Satyam as the worst scandalized company on the globe.

The basic questions to an intriguing mind are what tempted Satyam to undertake the downtrodden path of fraud and deceit, in its otherwise enviable record as the best-managed company? Could the compulsory requirements of the global capability index such as credibility status in business terms and the formality of submission of documents to claim compliance to the global CG norms as eligibility criteria, etc. lead to manoeuvre the scandalous initiatives to create a mask of excellence in the company's credentials?

How could a very small group of Satyam Family members along with few of their senior-level executives, and alleged role of the external financial consultants of world repute, manage to put an extremely opaque screen against exposition of the highly objectionable acts of fraud and deceit committed by the top management of the company? Similarly the fraudulent, scandalous deals, and activities of the Enrons of the world, the unceremonious downfall of the Lehman Brothers in the US, the Madoff misadventures are they in any way less serious than the drug mafias of the world over? One claims to be sane and reliable whereas the other declares his business as unsavoury, but the net objectivity is not far different, is it?

The Somalian pirates have made exploitation of the rich through brutal acts of kidnapping and high jacking the merchant ships for their basic needs of food and drugs, but it is limited to a particular area of activity, whereas the misdeeds of many world leaders in business have serious repercussions on the global economy, leading to catastrophic consequences. The acrimonious scenes we encounter in the political environment of most of the countries, the other scandals in high society lives of the glamour world in spite of global prescriptions on codes of conduct and ethical behaviour including the CG requirements in all walks of life are issues in ensuring a reliable and sustainable economic progress and world order seem like chasing a mirage.

Conclusions

We cannot deny the fact that today we are better informed, scientifically and technically better prepared and provided with security and safety against major maladies our ancestors could not face. The world has been converted to one location where everyone can experience through jet speed, communicate, and commute to every nook and corner of the world. We are today better acquainted with the nature and styles of lives of all around the globe. We understand each other in the world in a much clearer way than before. We share the advantages of all the technical and scientific process developments, researches, innovations all across the world. We are even trying to explore accessing resources from other planets in the universe.

What has been mentioned in the foregoing seems to be a little confusing on the developments as mentioned. The rub-off effect of the phenomenal advance in science and technology and their adoptions in the day-to-day life appear to be the over dependence on others for our essential and not so essential requirements, and consequent loss in self-confidence and ability to manage globalized complexity. But the mute question remains as to how do we manage sanctity in our global business avenues? If the global craze and complexity leads to unethical behaviour and conduct in managing our businesses, where do we pause and review, moderate, and proceed? The major focus of the Directors and the Indirectors seems to be saddled between global opportunities and scandalous temptations for misdemeanour.

Case Questions

1. What are the pitfalls in the current scope of Corporate Governance (CG) norms? What improvements and modifications do you suggest for effective implementation of CG?

2. Referring to the episodes in the above case study, which are the major reasons for the collapse of ethical standards of business conduct across the world in such cases?

3. In the Indian economic and business climate as of to date, what are the major corrections or moderations do you recommend in the duties and accountability of Independent Directors? Should they have overriding authorities on the main promoters? (Directors, etc.)

SECTION II

CASE STUDIES IN FINANCE MANAGEMENT

Financial Accounting, Direct/Indirect Taxation, Banking, and Insurance

6

Transfer Pricing in Cross Border Taxation

A Case Study of LG India and LG Electronics Korea

Learning Objectives

To understand transfer pricing. To apply transfer pricing to intangible assets/international trade/taxation. To analyse the circumstances under which LG became liable to pay tax. To analyse the methods adopted by the TPO to make LG India pay income tax in India. To gain knowledge and applications of various legal acts to support taxation of a foreign entity.

Synopsis

LG India is a subsidiary company of LG Electronics Korea, which had incurred advertisement, marketing, and sales promotion expenditure on behalf of LG Electronics Income Tax.

However the Transfer Pricing Officer (TPO) of the income tax department came up with a view that the said company had carried out foreign brand promotion in India for which it must have charged for such services to its foreign entity. And thus came up with a formula of cost plus 13% markup profit to determine the service price that LG should have charged to its foreign entity and pay income tax on such profits gained.

Indian Business Case Studies. Sandeep Pachpande, Asha Pachpande, and J A Kulkarni, Oxford University Press.
© ASM Group of Institutes, Pune, India 2022. DOI: 10.1093/oso/9780192869371.003.0006

Abbreviations used

1.	TP	Transfer Pricing
2.	TPO	Transfer Pricing Officer
3.	AMP	Advertisement, marketing and sales promotion expenses
4.	ALP	Arm's Length Price
5.	AE	Associated Enterprise
6.	AO	Assessing Officer
7.	DRP	Dispute Resolution Panel

Transfer Pricing

Transfer pricing (TP) has a significant role to play in terms of taxation of income from intangibles in case of inter-company TP in today's cross border world.

Multinational corporations have been tapping the Indian market through their local affiliates and naturally due to stiff competition they have increased their advertisement expenses manifold which has led to the growing importance of the key fore issue of TP, thereby creating income from intangibles and in turn taxation of the associated income.

The tax officials are overzealous to bring advertisement, marketing and sales promotion expense (AMP) in the tax bracket due to the number of multinational companies taking the shelter under TP adjustments.

With special reference to the LG Electronics case which is a wholly owned subsidiary of LG Electronics INC. Korea. As per the 'Technical Assistance and Royalty Agreement' executed on 1 July 2001, LG India was given a right to use the technical information, designs, drawings, and industrial property rights for the manufacture, marketing, sales, and services of the agreed products from LG Korea on payment of royalty at the rate of 1%. LG was also allowed to use the brand name and trademarks owned by LG Korea without payment of any royalty during the relevant period.

For the assessment year 2007–2008, the TPO found that the AMP Expenditure/Sales ratio of the taxpayer was 3.85 % against 1.39% of the two comparable companies. The TPO also held that the taxpayer promoted brand ownership by its foreign Associated Enterprise (AE) and therefore the taxpayer should have been compensated by the foreign AE for its excess AMP spend of 2.46%, that is, INR 1612.2 million. The TPO accordingly made a TP adjustment amounting to INR 1612.2 million.

The Dispute Resolution Panel (DRP), upholding the position taken by the TPO, further observed that the taxpayer should have charged markup on the cost of INR 1612.2 million incurred on rendering brand promotion services for LG Korea. Considering a rate of 10.5% on account of opportunity cost of the excessive funds deployed by the taxpayer and 2.5% as a compensation for the taxpayer's entrepreneurial efforts, the DRP held that the mark-up of 13% should have been applied on the amount proposed for adjustment based on the DRP'S directions the AO passed the order making an adjustment of INR 1827.1 million towards AMP expenditure incurred by the taxpayer on building for, and on behalf of LG Korea.

In relation to the decision of the Delhi High Court in the case of Maruti Suzuki Ltd, the Special Bench held that the decision on the merits of the case was not expressly or impliedly overruled by the Supreme Court.

In the said case the High Court had laid down certain principles for the determination of the Arms-Length Price (ALP) in respect of the international transaction of brand building for the foreign AE.

Thus the Special Bench held that the direction of the Supreme Court to the TPO inherently recognizes that there is a transaction of brand building between the taxpayer and the foreign AE, which is an international transaction as per Section 92B and the TPO has the jurisdiction to determine the ALP of such a transaction.

The Special Bench of the Income Tax Appellate Tribunal had taken a stand that the above AMP expenditure incurred by the Indian entity does amount to transaction on the following grounds:

1. Display of brand in the advertisements coupled with proportionately higher AMP spend by the taxpayer indicated an oral or tacit understanding between the taxpayer and the foreign AE regarding promotion by the taxpayer.
2. It made a special reference to Section 92F(iv) of the Act in which it is mentioned that the transaction could be 'express' or 'Oral'.

3. The present case clearly states that the Indian Associate Enterprise had prominently displayed the brand of its foreign AE in its advertisement that gave rise to its expenditure more than proportionate as in the ordinary course of the transactions made in India.
4. The taxpayer has clearly provided services that resulted into higher AMP, which cannot be a free luncheon and must have been charged for such services to its foreign enterprise which gives an indication of giving birth to an international transaction.

LG India View

1. The taxpayer contended that Section 92CA(2A) Of the Act providing for such suo moto assumption of jurisdiction by the TPO was inserted from 1 June 2011 and Section 92CA(2B) of the Act having retrospective effect from 1 June 2002 was inserted in 2012, these two sub-sections cannot come to the rescue of the TPO because none of them were in existence at the time of its passing of the Act which was only on 29 October 2010.
2. The taxpayer also upheld its view regarding the brightest line test or the ARM'S length AMP expenditure test (which formed the basis of deciding the AMP expenditure) cannot be a method that can be adopted which was not mentioned in Section 92C of the Income Tax Act.
3. The taxpayer also holds the view that the AMP expenditure incurred are fully deductible under Section 37(1) of the Income Tax Act, 1961 and there is no question of determining the ALP in this regards and such conditions are duly satisfied even if the foreign AE gets some incidental benefit out of such expenditure and such TP adjustment will reduce the amount of deduction in turn resulting to end up paying more tax which is otherwise allowable under Section 37(1) of the Act.
4. It is also of the view that the decisions based on erstwhile Section 37(3B) of the Act, that the expenditure incurred directly 'in connection with' and not 'for promotion of sales' should not be put in the same basket as AMP expenditure. Therefore bonus/commission paid to dealers/sales agent does not constitute AMP expenditure.

Special Bench of the Income Tax Tribunal View

1. The TPO had made assumptions based on the understanding that the Indian Entity (LG India) which is a subsidiary of the LG Electronics Korea must have been adequately compensated by the foreign company because of the brand promotions done by its Indian counterpart and this certainly amounted to international transaction which is liable for TP taxation in India.

2. The Special Bench had the view that international pricing transaction is an altogether different ball game and it has to be independently viewed to be a separate transaction with no regular provision to be applied and the present section 92 of the Income Tax Act do not apply because of various amendments to Section 92.

3. Bonus and commission paid to dealers/sales agent does not constitute AMP expenditure; the Special Bench had accepted this view.

Such assumptions can sometimes be erroneous as assessing the income of an entity earns cannot be done by way of backward calculation as the taxpayer has not made any mention of the cost that it had incurred.

Resultant

Understand the concept of TP
Understand criteria for taxation of foreign entities
Ability to apply TP to intangible assets
Analysis of cross border negotiations for the purposes of taxation
Differentiate between taxation of tangible and intangible asset

Conclusions

The place of TP in the determination of income tax on intangibles in case of inter-company TP in international finance. Multinational corporations incur advertisement expenses manifold leading to the growing importance of the key role of TPO, thereby creating income from intangibles and in turn taxation of the associated income. Tax officials are anxious to bring AMP in the tax bracket due to the number of multinational companies taking the shelter under TP adjustments. LG India was a cornerstone case study of the above phenomenon bringing MNCs in the tax net.

Case Questions

1. Do promotional expenses incurred by the Indian companies licensees of the trademark enhance the value of a trademark which is legally owned by the Associated Enterprise (foreign company)?

2. Do you think that the TPO was right in making a conclusion that the Indian company must have been adequately compensated by the Associated Enterprise (LG Electronics Korea)?

3. Do you think the 13% markup determined by the Dispute Resolution Panel was based on scientific basis? Or, is there another method that should have been adopted in the above case? Or was there ever a markup profit earned in the first place?

4. Whether the facts and the circumstances of the case, determine the AO's proper justification in making the transfer pricing adjustment in relation to advertisement, marketing and sales promotion expenditure incurred by the taxpayer?

7

A Case Study on Direct Taxation

Learning Objectives

The primary purpose of taxation is to raise revenue to meet huge public expenditures. Most governmental activities must be financed by taxation. But it is not the only goal. In other words, taxation policy has some non-revenue objectives and hence collection of due taxes is critical for the government.

The learning objective of this case study is to understand the significance of transfer pricing with the perspective of taxation of income, during intercompany transfers.

Synopsis

M/S Shell India and Shell Gas BV

The transfer pricing has a significant role to play in terms of taxation of income from intangibles in case of intercompany transfer pricing, in today's world.

With special reference to the Shell case which is a wholly owned subsidiary of the Royal Dutch Shell Group.

The Royal Dutch Shell Group was created in February 1907 through the amalgamation of two rival companies: Royal Dutch Petroleum Company and the 'Shell' Transport and Trading Company Ltd of the United Kingdom.

Case Details

Shell India Markets Pvt Ltd (Shell India) is a wholly owned subsidiary of the Royal Dutch Shell Group of Companies. Shell India (the taxpayer)

Indian Business Case Studies. Sandeep Pachpande, Asha Pachpande, and J A Kulkarni, Oxford University Press.
© ASM Group of Institutes, Pune, India 2022. DOI: 10.1093/oso/9780192869371.003.0007

had issued equity shares to its non-resident associated enterprises (AEs) at face value. The Transfer Pricing Officer (TPO) alleged short receipt of consideration for issue of shares and made an adjustment for the difference between the arm's length price (ALP) consideration (as computed by the TPO) and the consideration based on face value (as had been received by the taxpayer). The TPO also added an interest amount on the short receipt. Aggrieved, the taxpayer filed a writ petition before the High Court of Bombay (HC) on the issue of jurisdiction, that is, the jurisdiction of revenue to bring to tax amount received on capital account, viz., issue of equity shares to its AEs under Chapter X of the Indian Income-tax Act, 1961 (the Act).

Shell India had issued 870 million shares to Shell Gas BV in March 2009, at Rs.10 a share. However, the Income Tax department was of the view that the shares were grossly undervalued, and it valued them at Rs. 180 a share. Thus the department added the difference to the taxable income of Shell India. Furthermore, the Income Tax department had issued a show-cause notice adding another Rs.3,100 crore to Shell India's income for 2008–2009 in another transfer pricing case. Being aggrieved, the company moved the Bombay High Court, challenging the tax notice.

The tax authorities argued that the deal is a transfer pricing arrangement by which the share issued are undervalued and hence the company is liable to pay tax on the income generated out of it. The tax authorities also asked for tax on the interest the Anglo-Dutch Oil Company would have earned in cases of underpriced transfer of shares.

On the contrary the Shell Plc argued that the foreign parent's equity infusion into its subsidiary is not liable to be taxed, the same being Foreign Direct Investment which cannot be taxed. Shell Plc also denied the argument of the tax authority saying that the price of the share was perfectly valued and not undervalued.

The bench of Justices Bombay High Court decided on a petition filed by Shell India Markets. The Court ruled in the favour of the Shell Plc on the ground that, under the provisions of transfer pricing the issuance of shares by an Indian Company to its foreign partner is not taxable. The judgment has specified that transfer pricing laws cannot be imposed on shares issued to a foreign parent. It has been the practice of multinationals to fund its subsidiary by issuing shares, court viewed it as capital transaction thus not covered under the rule of transfer pricing.

The HC held that the jurisdiction to apply Chapter X of the Act would be occasion only when income arises out of an international transaction and such income is chargeable to tax under the Act.

Further, the HC held that the fact that the taxpayer chose not to declare issue of shares to its AEs in Form 3CEB as in its understanding it fell outside the scope of Chapter X of the Act, now stands vindicated by the decision of the HC in the case of Vodafone India Services Private Limited. Moreover, the HC clarified that mere non-filing of Form 3CEB on the part of the taxpayer would not give jurisdiction to the revenue to tax an amount which it does not have jurisdiction to. In India it incorporated a co. by the name Shell India Markets Pvt Ltd. as an Indian co. and was controlling Shell India (the Child) by Shell Gas BV (the parent) a foreign company. Shell Gas BV was holding 100% stake in Shell India. To intensify its business proceedings in India, Shell India came out with issue of equity shares in the year 2009. And the stage was well set for the IT department to make its entry when all of such shares were bought by Shell Gas BV (Foreign Co.), that is, nothing but Foreign (In)Direct Investment of Rs. 87 Crores, the area of conflict being that all such shares were issued at Rs. 10/Share (18 US Cents). And here comes the twist in the story, the entry was late but it was the ultimate and latest thing that happened when IT department sent a notice in January 2013 to Shell Gas BV depicting that the Shell India was undervalued in connection with the equity issue. In March 2009 the shares issue to Shell Gas BV were issued at Rs.10/share, but the income-tax authorities peg the deal at Rs.183/share. It would challenge a tax department notice which claims that it underpriced a sale of shares to an overseas group company by $2.7 billion.

Protagonist

Contentions of Petitioner

Taxpayer contended that as per Section 92(1) of the Act: Prerequisite for application of this section is that the income should arise from an international transaction. In this case, no income arises from issue of equity shares and capital receipts are not income under the Act unless specifically provided for (Section 2(24) (xvi) of the Act).

The taxpayer also upheld its view that the order of the TPO/DRP demonstrates that shortfall in premium on issue of shares is not taxable in as much as amount received by the petitioner on account of share premium has not been taxed. If there is any impact of income on account of business restructuring/reorganizing, then only such income would be subjected to tax as and when it arises whether in present or in future. In this case, such a contingency does not arise as there is no impact on income which would be chargeable to tax due to issue of shares (Section 92B of the Act).

Section 92(2) of the Act: The objective is to ensure that profits are not understated nor losses overstated by disclosing higher cost or expenditure, than the benefit received. Hence it has no application in the present case.

The view was taken by revenue that if the petitioner had got the extra premium he would have invested it somewhere and would have earned additional income is based on pure guesswork and is not admissible.

Contentions of Revenue

Section 92(1) of the Act: Uses the word 'Any income arising from an International Transaction'. This indicates that the income of either party to the transaction could be subject matter of tax and not the income of resident only. Under Chapter X of the Act, real income concept has no application otherwise the words would have been 'actual income'. Section 2(24) of the Act: Income as defined is an inclusive definition and it does not prohibit taxing capital receipts as income.

Section 2(47) of the Act: The issue of shares is a transfer within the meaning of the term 'income'. The forgoing of premium on the part of the petitioner amounts to extinguishment/ relinquishment of a right to receive fair market value and Clauses (c) and (e) of the Explanation (i) to Section 92B of the Act: The meaning of international transaction as given would include even capital account transaction within its scope.

A conjoint reading of Section 92(1) of the Act along with Section 92(2) of the Act: indicate that what is being brought to tax is not share premium but the cost incurred by the petitioner in passing on a benefit to its holding company by issue of shares at a premium less than ALP.

The order of the TPO/DRP demonstrates that premium on issue of share is not taxable in as much as amounts received by petitioner on account of share premium have not been taxed. The petitioner itself had submitted to the jurisdiction of Chapter X of the Act by filing/submitting Form 3-CEB, declaring the ALP.

Under Act, the income is taxable when it accrues or arises or when it is deemed to accrue or arise and not only when it is received. Therefore, even if an amount is not actually received, yet in case income has arisen or deemed to arise, then the same is chargeable to tax. Thus, income forgone is also subject to tax. Chapter X of the Act is a complete code by itself and not merely a machinery provision to compute the ALP and applies wherever the ALP is to be determined by the AO.

The passing on of benefit by the petitioner to its holding company would fall under the head 'Income' from other sources under Section 56(1) of the Act.

In the Shell case, the tax office alleged that the company's Indian unit under-priced shares transferred to the parent by about $2.5 billion, demanding tax on the interest the Anglo-Dutch oil company would have earned. The income-tax department had sought to add Rs 15,220 crore to Shell India's taxable income.

Shell India had issued shares to parent Shell Gas BV at Rs 10 apiece in the 2008–2009 financial year. The tax department contested this valuation and estimated it at Rs 183 per share. The difference resulting from the revaluation of shares was treated as income in the hands of Shell India.

Conclusions

This case study meticulously explains the intricacies of taxation during intercompany transfer pricing transactions.

The petitioner argued that the view of the revenue regarding investment of extra premium somewhere would earn additional income was inadmissible.

While the Income Tax department argued that the valuation of Rs 10 per share offered by Shell India to its parent Shell Gas BV, was heavily underpriced and estimated at Rs 183 per share. According to them the difference resulting from their evaluation of shares was an income in the hands of Shell India which had to be taxed.

It has to be noted that tax is the major source of revenue for the government, the development of any country's economy largely depends on the tax structure it has adopted. A taxation structure which facilitates the easy of doing business and having no chance for tax evasion brings prosperity to a country's economy. On the other hand taxation structure which has provisions for tax evasion and the one which does not facilitate ease of doing business slows down the growth of country's economy.

Case Questions

1. Whether the facts and the circumstances of the case, determine the AO's proper justification, valuing the issued shares as underpriced, in making the transfer pricing adjustment in relation to Share Price Income incurred by the taxpayer?

2. The court decision came as in favour of Shell India challenged the order of the Income Tax Appellate Tribunal, to circumvent transfer pricing norms, though it was an international transaction wherein there was no arm's length dealing between the related entities. Discuss whether the court decision is in favour of Shell India Company's reputation and result in increase in foreign investors.

3. Should the transfer pricing policy be seriously reviewed? What happens if a multinational company issue shares to overseas holding co. and later on issue shares to others at a premium, will it not be passing gain without and tax on such gain?

8

The Common Tragedy in the Non-Banking Financial Corporations (NBFC)

A Case Study on the 'Infrastructure Leasing & Financial Services' Episode

Learning Objectives

Corporate governance and its implications are not just restricted to board room discussions especially in case of financial institutions. Reason for this is they implicate the financial markets due to which they have larger public repercussions. This creates external implications as money invested in financial markets is done by the general public and not by the financial institution. So governance plays an important role within and outside the firms.

Synopsis

Financial woes of the Indian economy continue in spite of taking strong measures. In 2009 Satyam fiasco rocked the stock markets and similar type of incident has taken place in 2018. Stock markets were flying high and bullish trend was present in markets in September 2018 up to third week. Then the markets showed a downward trend and speculations were made regarding the reasons for the same.

With the future stability of the Indian financial system on the line, executives running a giant infrastructure lender gathered at the company's glassy, modernist headquarters in Mumbai and hammered out an ambitious restructuring plan in September last week to manage a $12.6 billion debt burden after a string of defaults.

Indian Business Case Studies. Sandeep Pachpande, Asha Pachpande, and J A Kulkarni, Oxford University Press.
© ASM Group of Institutes, Pune, India 2022. DOI: 10.1093/oso/9780192869371.003.0008

Except that they weren't really calling the shots anymore. The very next day, the government in New Delhi authorized a move to sweep in and seize control of Infrastructure Leasing & Financial Services Ltd. (IL&FS), a vast conglomerate that raised billions of dollars in the corporate bond market and powered the nation's public project building boom.

The stunning move, more typical of China's command-and-control economy than a free-wheeling democracy like India, caught investors by surprise.

The decision to oust the company's board was taken after the government had quietly reached out, at least two days earlier, to former bureaucrats and current bankers to orchestrate a board coup, according to people familiar with the matter. The government had been monitoring the lender for two weeks, one of the people said.

Following a series of meetings in September and months after the first defaults by the systemically important lender, the ministry was worried about the multiple shocks to the financial markets that would follow from IL&FS's collapse.

'The restoration of confidence of the money, debt and capital markets, the banks and financial institutions in the credibility and financial solvency of the IL&FS Group is of utmost importance for the financial stability of capital and financial markets,' the government said in a statement

The Case Details

What Is IL&FS?

IL&FS is one of the oldest infrastructure services had in the past helped out many projects in India. To their credit to name a few Chenani-Nashri Tunnel (or Patnitop Tunnel) in Udhampur Built at the foot of the Himalayan Mountains, the 9 km-long Patni top tunnel connects the districts of Chenani and Nashri. The project involved an investment of Rs 37.2bn ($723m). Also many road projects have been built by them. The investors in this include LIC and SBI. It has a long list of subsidiaries.

The case is of peculiar nature of IL&FS. It is supposed to be a private company, which acts like a quasi-government arm because it lends to the infrastructure sector and has a lot of big government companies and banks as shareholders. More importantly, it is both a lending in-stitution and an execution company. It has bid, won, and taken on projects under various subsidiaries, and which in turn have raised debt financing both from the parent and from the market. The sub-sidiaries were needed to be created because the government regula-tions mandate that each concession-based infrastructure project needs a separate entity because loans are taken specifically to that entity and project. With IL&FS taking on so many projects, it became a highly opaque structure with the government as a partner in most of its projects, which gave many the feeling of comfort that the risks were underwritten by the government. And it had a management team, which successfully hid the rising crisis and tried to bury it under the carpet until it could no longer do so.

A loan of a ₹1,000 crore from the Small Industries Development Bank of India (SIDBI) on 13 September had been defaulted. The person who was heading the firm Mr Ravi Parthasarathy quit the company giving health reasons. On 17 September, rating agency ICRA downgraded IL&FS's credit rating to default after it failed to meet repayment obliga-tions of ₹12,000 crore in short-term and long-term borrowings.

With cash crunch and falling stock markets the company started missing on payments. Commercial papers payments were missed and suddenly the markets and lenders started getting the indication that all is not well. Banks, mutual and pension fund managers, insurers, and indi-viduals are bracing for further losses. Among the concerns for investors is that IL&FS has made loans to its own units. The company is also in default on short-term borrowings known as inter-corporate deposits.

Then the news of DSP Mutual Fund selling DHFL's one-year ₹300 crore paper at 11% and the subsequent fear of a contagion effect spooked the market. DSP Investment Managers Pvt Ltd later clarified it had no credit issue with DHFL and was just trying to reduce its portfolio ma-turity. The DHFL management also said that it had not defaulted on any bonds or repayment, nor had there been any instance of delay on repay-ment of any liability. The management of DHFL said it did not have any exposure to IL&FS.

Reserve Bank of India (RBI) smelt something fishy and an audit was initiated. The report cited many lapses and in meantime the bonds on which payments were due did not take place. This created panic and the secrets came out in to the open. At this point the share market also saw a downfall with cash crunch and prices started falling down.

The shareholding and the projects and the dozens of subsidiaries made things even more complicated for rating agencies as well as auditors, though they should have been more vigilant given the problems that all infrastructure companies are facing. To be fair to the credit rating agencies, they had flagged off a warning, though inexplicably, perhaps lulled by the blue-chip projects, its partners, and its quasi-government nature; they failed to downgrade the debt early enough until the defaults actually started.

Outcome

On 1 October 2018 the government announced that it is taking control of the management of IL&FS, whose loans and debentures have been downgraded to default status by rating agency ICRA. The Mumbai National Company Law Tribunal—a quasi-judicial body that decides on issues relating to Indian companies—allowed India's ministry of corporate affairs to replace the company's board with a new one.

The existing management of IL&FS has been replaced with a new six-member board, which will be helmed by Mr Uday Kotak, managing director of Kotak Mahindra Bank.

Other members include Mr Vineet Nayyar, executive vice chairman of the IT services company Tech Mahindra; Mr GN Bajpai, former chief of India's market regulator Securities and Exchange Board of India, former ICICI Bank Chairman Mr GC Chaturvedi, and former IAS officers Mr Malini Shankar and Mr Nanda Kishore.

But unlike Lehman, the government has already indicated that IL&FS is not going to be allowed to collapse. The rescue plan is already in place and its shareholders like LIC and SBI are ready to give it enough money to meet its repayment obligations.

However, the IL&FS case should be a wake-up call for the government precisely for the reason that it reached a stage of collapse without anyone spotting the problem early on. Unlike the case of banks, where the RBI had spotted the problems early on, and where it had prodded them to recognize the bad debts and clean up balance sheets, the IL&FS case shows the gaps that exist in our financial systems especially asset-liability mismatches or the credit risk in the NBFC space even now, which need to be plugged quickly.

Future

What are the lessons going forward? One is of course that it makes little sense to have an NBFC, which also is in the business of actually executing infrastructure projects. A pure lending agency would have probably been monitored more closely by the RBI. Equally, execution agencies about to get into cash flow trouble are far easier to spot because they are also not raising debt as a lending NBFC.

Another point is that the government does need to figure out why so many infrastructure projects run into cash flow and other financial problems (which in turn creates problems for their lenders). This is a bigger problem because infrastructure is a long gestation business, while finances raised are for shorter tenures thus causing asset liability and cash flow mismatches.

Finally, it might make the best sense to slowly wind up the IL&FS business after selling off its debt and paying off its asset instead of letting it exist with a rap on the knuckles.

The tide seems to have turned in favour of commercial banks: the liquidity crunch following the IL&FS crisis has pushed corporate borrowers away from the bond markets, back to banks.

Data released by the RBI on 24 October shows non-food credit growth at over a four-year high of 14.5% year-on-year (y-o-y) for the fortnight ended 12 October. In absolute terms, non-food credit grew from ₹78.15 trillion in the fortnight ended 13 October 2017 to ₹89.47 trillion in the 12 October 2018 fortnight.

Bankers are upbeat about the growth in credit and said corporate borrowers are returning as bond markets turn risk averse.

'The gap between bank lending rates and the borrowing rates from the bond market has considerably narrowed now. Moreover, in some cases, bank loans are turning out to be cheaper than bonds,' said P.K. Gupta, managing director, State Bank of India (SBI).

The current credit apprehension in the bond markets has been beneficial to banks as borrowers have started preferring bank loans over bonds, according to Mr Ajay Manglunia, head (fixed income advisory), Edelweiss Financial Services.

'Banks have cashed in on the opportunity presented by the falling risk appetite of the bond market after the IL&FS crisis. Investors are going slow on investing in financial companies and that has led to higher spreads for other bond issuers as well at this moment,' said Mr Manglunia. He said that AA-rated borrower can raise funds from the bond market at 9.5–10% now, up from 8.5% a year ago.

Conclusions

The IL&FS crisis has thrown the business of Non-Banking Financial Companies (NBFCs) in disarray. With liquidity becoming an issue, the parallels between an approaching winter and the chill that is setting in on small business financing are being talked about in great detail.

Lenders are not sure if there are any more skeletons in the closet and every payment and repayment schedule of an NBFC is being scrutinized threadbare for any signs of distress. Mutual funds, which made a killing in the last three years, have also decided to go slow on exposure to NBFCs. As a result, there is suddenly a severe liquidity crisis in the sector and this is bound to have an impact on small businesses in the country. SMEs in the country have become reliant on NBFCs to fund their needs and there is a fear that with liquidity being an issue, these small businesses would find it very tough to raise money. As a result, thousands of jobs would now be at risk. The task for the new board, then, is cut out—to raise long-term equity to pull the company out of the woods.

Case Questions

1. Government has reacted to the situation but can it solve the problem. The shadow bank is a financial behemoth with assets in excess of Rs 1.15 lakh crore ($16 billion) and debt of Rs 91,000 crore.

2. What should be the precautions to be taken in future from audit view to ensure such repercussions do not take place?

9

Embracing and Pursuing Change

A Case Study of an Insurance Company

Learning Objectives

This case study focuses upon AEGON in the UK, part of the AEGON Group, one of the world's largest life insurance and pensions companies. AEGON owns pensions, life insurance, and asset management and adviser business in the UK. The case study illustrates the success that embracing and pursuing change has brought to AEGON in the UK. The company was facing a strategic drift. To study the reason of low level of awareness impact on its ability to achieve its ambitions. To know about the imposing of prices by the government on goods which had led the reduction in profitability. It is helping AEGON move towards its goal of becoming the best long-term savings and protection business within the UK.

Synopsis

With the changing expectations of customers, organizations constantly need to adapt to remain competitive. When faced with such pressures for change, managers may look for situations which are familiar to them. This may involve improving the ways in which they operate, but only little by little. This is called incremental change. The danger is that improving little by little might not be enough. They need to adapt to all of the bigger changes in the environment of that business as well. If they don't what happens is strategic drift.

Indian Business Case Studies. Sandeep Pachpande, Asha Pachpande, and J A Kulkarni, Oxford University Press.
© ASM Group of Institutes, Pune, India 2022. DOI: 10.1093/oso/9780192869371.003.0009

Introduction

The AEGON Group has 27,000 employees and over 25 million customers worldwide. Its major markets are in the USA and Netherlands. Since 1994, the UK has become another major and increasingly important market. In 1994 AEGON bought a large stake in Scottish Equitable was a strong brand with a heritage that went back to the 1830s. Since then AEGON's UK business has grown both organically and by acquiring other businesses.

As most of the acquired companies kept their existing identities, awareness of AEGON in the UK remained relatively low. AEGON realized that such low levels of awareness could impact on its ability to achieve its ambitions. Therefore, it needed to combine the global strength of its parent with the experience and reputation of the domestic company brands, like Scottish Equitable, that made up AEGON in the UK.

External Factors Influencing Change

One of the main challenges for decision makers is to understand the environment in which they are operating. They can then identify key issues which they need to respond to. Understanding these key issues improves decision-taking and reduces uncertainty. Few industries have experienced as many changes in their external environment in recent years as financial services.

Thinking ahead and saving for retirement is a concept that is sometimes difficult for people to understand. In the UK, life expectancy has risen in recent years so people can expect to be retired for longer. In many instances, individuals have not planned properly for retirement and there may be a shortfall in the amount of money available. There is also a drive by the government to reduce dependency on the state in old age. Added to this many companies have introduced new, less expensive pension schemes or insisted on employee pension contributions where they did not in the past. These factors mean people have to make decisions to invest properly at an earlier stage of their working lives. Investing in the future helps people to prepare in advance for old age. The benefits of such an investment are only realized years later.

The Case Details

The life insurance and pensions industry, in which AEGON operates, has had a poor reputation in recent years. Some organizations have been accused of 'mis-selling' by not providing consumers with the best product for their needs. To prevent similar situations arising in the future the Financial Services Authority (FSA) has put significant amounts of regulation on the industry.

Financial services products are often difficult to understand. People do not always feel equipped to choose between the range of financial products and services and are not sure where to seek support and advice. In addition, falling values on the Stock Exchange have affected the investment return on some products, such as mortgage endowments. For some people this means that the product they bought has not delivered the financial return they expected. All this has created uncertainty in the financial services industry.

The industry has also been characterized by intense competition. AEGON is in competition with organizations which sell directly to consumers and which are better known in the UK. AEGON distributes its products and services to customers mainly through financial advisers. AEGON, as a reputable company, has had to address and overcome these industry-wide problems to remain competitive.

Reasons for Change

AEGON had historically been successful but government-imposed price controls had reduced profitability. Compared to its competitors, AEGON was not well known by consumers. It had developed good products and services and had a good reputation with distributors, particularly in the area of pensions which were a key strength of Scottish Equitable. However, it was not as well recognised in areas other than pensions. Often these other areas, such as offshore investment products, were more profitable. If consumers are to invest in a product long term, they need to know more about the organization they are dealing with.

They need to recognize the brand and understand more about the brand values that it represents. As AEGON traded under a number of brand names it was not always easy for financial advisers and consumers to recognize the breadth and depth of the company in the UK.

How to Move Forward?

With a new Chief Executive (CEO) in place, AEGON underwent a discovery phase. The purpose of this was to find out what it had to do to meet the CEO's goal. This goal was to build 'the best long-term savings and protection business in the UK'. This time of discovery focused on three key questions:

1. What do we stand for in the UK?
2. What do we want to stand for in the UK?
3. What should we be doing about it?

Brand Audit

To answer these questions AEGON undertook a brand audit. This audit looked at two aspects:

1. The company internally.
2. How the organization was positioned externally.

The purpose of the audit was to find out more information about the organization. They helped AEGON to provide a more informed approach to the decisions that were needed to start the process of change. The audit showed that AEGON was solidly placed within the market. Its staff was known for their considerable expertise, innovation, and clarity of communication. The external audit also helped to discover where AEGON was positioned in relation to its competitors. People who were aware of AEGON saw it as being a refreshing and different organization. However, there was evidence that people were confused about the breadth of what AEGON did because it traded under a number of different company brands.

Creating a New Culture Is a Key Part of Change Process

Culture refers to the personality and attitude of an organization. It also includes the shared beliefs, values, and behaviour of the employees. These determine the ways in which the organization and its people make decisions and solve problems. The goal of AEGON's CEO helped to provide a vision for change. Financial objectives were important as the path for future developments depended upon these. It was also important to create more clarity about who AEGON was. With limited awareness of AEGON in the UK, it was important to explain what it had to offer, how big the organization was within the UK, and how strong it was globally. At the heart of this strategy was the need to:

1. Simplify financial services and provide more customer focus. It was important that consumers understood more precisely what they were buying, as well as the benefits and services they received.
2. Develop the workforce. The objective was to develop the skills needed within the business to help it change. AEGON also created opportunities for progression from one job to another in a way that provided individuals with a coherent career path.
3. Create a more distinct presence within the marketplace. This involved refreshing the AEGON brand in a way that made it more distinctive from its competitors and more attractive to customers.

A Behavioural Framework

In order to help embed this culture, AEGON developed a behaviour framework to support its brand values. This was designed to influence how people at all levels within the organization could work and make decisions. These behaviours emphasize the values of the organization. They have helped to build AEGON's culture and have also influenced its performance. AEGON also introduced a Management Development Programme, supported by a leading management college.

The eight behaviours are:

1. Think customer	5. Decisive action
2. Embrace change	6. Work together
3. Encourage excellence	7. Learn and grow
4. Act with integrity	8. Relate and communicate.

'Think customer' is about 'ensuring that the customer's needs are at the heart of our business, informing actions, decisions and behaviours'. For senior managers this means keeping the customer's experience at the heart of what AEGON does. Other managers and professionals are encouraged to 'innovate with your customers in mind'. All staff are encouraged to keep to commitments made to customers by doing 'what you say you will, when you say you will'.

Implementing the Change

Before the change, consumers were confused about who AEGON was, what it did, and how it fitted together. The audit had shown that global scale was important but so was local expertise. In the past, the AEGON brand had not been heavily promoted alongside Scottish Equitable or the other brand that it traded under. The brand strategy helped to reposition the brand within the industry. Now the association with AEGON is much stronger. For example, Scottish Equitable is now AEGON Scottish Equitable—reflecting both local knowledge and global power. All the brands are now carry a new common look which is refreshing and different. This, along with the values and behaviours, is helping to make the brand 'refreshingly different'.

Impacts of Change

The changes affected the organization both internally and externally. Within the organization, they influenced not only how people behaved but also how they communicated. The organization has become more focused on the customer. The emphasis is on making information clearer for the customer to understand and the company easier to do business with. To help embed the values and behaviours, AEGON established a new relationship with Shirley Robertson, the famous yachtswoman and the only British female athlete to have won gold medal at consecutive Olympic Games. By associating Aegon with an individual who embodies similar values, it was able to bring the values and behaviours to life for staff.

However, AEGON had to develop the brand and its reputation. It did this in a number of ways:

1. External promotion campaigns emphasized the relationship between the Scottish Equitable and AEGON. This helped to reinforce the local knowledge and the global power of AEGON in the UK.
2. The CEO talked to the media about the need of change. The refreshing of the brand internally and externally resulted in strong positive feedback.
3. AEGON has launched new and innovative products. For example, the five for Life annuity has helped to change the way in which consumers can look at their retirement income. It provides more certainty about levels of incomes for the consumer, with AEGON providing levels of return promised and being responsible for any risks associated with doing so.

Today the AEGON brand has a position from which it is influencing the financial services industry. It has posted record results with significant growth in underlying earnings. It has also increased its new business across a mix of profitable products and services, reflecting its continued strength.

Conclusions

Change is continuous. The process of change is a journey. External factors will always be there to influence business organization. AEGON responded to those factors by simplifying, clarifying, and strengthening its brand in the UK. As organizations change, their patterns of behaviour and business culture develop. For AEGON, this is a cycle in which the business uses its knowledge to learn from its experiences. This has helped AEGON as an organization to move positively towards achieving its full potential and to remain competitive in an increasingly difficult market (Business Case Studies LLP).

Case Questions

1. What factors have led AEGON to crisis?

2. State the strategy adopted by AGEON to come back in market with full potential.

3. Do really the process of change has helped AEGON to occupy market world?

SECTION III

MULTIDISCIPLINARY CASE STUDIES IN MARKETING, STRATEGY, OPERATIONS

*Marketing Management, Strategic Management
Mergers and Acquisitions and Operations Strategy*

10

Tata Motors—The Indian Auto Giant

A Case Study on Perennial Issues at the Indian Auto Giant TAMO

Learning Objectives

What Tata Motors (TAMO) has managed to do is something we seldom see in the automotive industry. They have managed to build a new identity and are becoming an inspirational brand. This case of TAMO highlights the impact of social media campaign and celebrity endorsement on the sales and brand awareness of Tata Tiago, a hatchback car offered by TAMO. It focuses on some areas like the methodologies adopted by TAMO before finalizing machining facilities for car designing, pricing strategies, etc. The factors like aesthetics, looks of car models, etc. influence purchasing decisions of female buyers. This case will also help us to understand various marketing strategies and approaches adopted by TAMO to aggressively stand strong in the hatchback cars market.

Synopsis

This case tries to understand and analyse the marketing strategy adopted by TAMO for Tiago. The practice of segmenting, targeting, and positioning of products with right choice of channels to reach out to the targeted segment is used by TAMO to strengthen the market position of their other products. The below case highlights how the designers at TAMO used various platforms for developing car models right from traditional clay miniatures to life-size models to digitization of final shapes before finalizing the machining facilities. The great success behind TAMO designs is considering the role and mindset of female buyers as

Indian Business Case Studies. Sandeep Pachpande, Asha Pachpande, and J A Kulkarni, Oxford University Press.
© ASM Group of Institutes, Pune, India 2022. DOI: 10.1093/oso/9780192869371.003.0010

well as drivers which they focus more. This case study gives us insight about how TAMO turned the wheels of fortune and re-imagined the way we look at cars!

Introduction

At the TAMO design studio in Pune, a group of qualified and experienced people play around with clay, making models of cars throughout the day. Some are miniatures but then others are life-size. The clay is special; when heated to 65 degrees centigrade, it is soft and malleable. Cooled to room temperature, it becomes harder and lends itself to scraping and sculpting with knives. Often, the team works on four models at a time, moulding and taking images to digitize the final shape. It helps TAMO design better cars and also helps answer a larger question.

The other is handcrafting a full-size car out of metal and plastic. That's not futuristic technology at work; rather it is going back to the basics of car designing, something TAMO took almost two decades to learn. The handcrafted model is great for getting feedback before machining facilities are finalized. Then there are the finer details that Bose points out—colours must match across material, metals, and plastic, and they should look similar from different angles.

Role of Women Drivers

The company also learnt that women drivers are impressed by such attention to detail. They also like utilities inside the car. Mayank Pareek, President of TAMO for passenger vehicles, says: 'We have done the hard work in reinvigorating and recasting Tata Motors' products with an eye on customer preferences.

Women are important influencers when it comes to the purchase of a car. They are also 17 per cent of our customer base.' The result is Tata's new car Tiago, a hatchback priced at Rs 3.20 lakh which, in its third month, outsells every other model from the Tata stable. Launched in April 2016, 4,205 Tiagos were sold in June, 22% more than the previous month's sales.

With pending bookings exceeding 23,000, the Tiago can easily notch up higher numbers in the coming months. With great looks, interiors, and great audio to wow the customer, Tiago hopes to remake TAMOs' passenger cars division and take the company back to among the top three in Indian passenger cars market, as India MD Guenter Butschek, said in his message to shareholders in the company's annual report. As of June, TAMO is ranked No. 5 in market share.

Uphill Climb

Tiago may be outperforming other Tata models, but across industry it is perched at No. 17 in the monthly car sales. Two other recent hatchback launches, Renault's Kwid and Datsun's Redi-GO, have scorched a pace. Kwid, launched in September 2015, sold almost 10,000 units in June, with bookings exceeding 1.5 lakh. Redi-GO, launched after Tiago, has notched up 10,000 bookings already.

TAMO is hopeful that the features packed and aggressively priced Tiago—it is priced between Kwid and Maruti's Alto K10—will shake up the hatchback segment, which accounts for 50% of all car sales. Tiago is critical to TAMOs' relevance in the car business. There's reason for that: in 2015–2016, the passenger vehicles sales of TAMO had fallen by 7%. While the consolidated TAMO operation (with JLR) had reported a profit in excess of Rs 11,000 crore for 2015–2016, the Indian operation—including passenger and commercial vehicles—contributed only Rs 234.23 crore, or a little over 2%. The underperformance is a reflection of little working for TAMO on the new products front. Zest, a compact sedan, and Bolt, a premium hatchback, the first two Tata cars that were built with the philosophy of targeting individual buyers rather than fleet owners, have not seen the kind of success anticipated.

The passenger vehicles segment recorded a 37% growth in sales in June over May. However, apart from the Tiago, growth has come from the old work horses, the Indica and the Indigo. These are the fleet cars, and precisely the image that the company is trying to erase. The Indica sold 2,223 units in June after a lacklustre 904 in May and the Indigo sold 1,960 units in June, a 232% growth over its May sales.

Part of the Solution

While June delivered good numbers for TAMO, there was bad news elsewhere. Lionel Messi, the company's brand ambassador, almost ran aground his endorsement value. Messi, after a sterling run to the final in Copa America, missed his shot in the penalty shootout as Argentina lost to Chile. He promptly announced his retirement from international football. Then the star and his father were convicted of tax fraud in Spain with prospects of a suspended jail term—leading to speculation that Messi may leave his Spanish club Barcelona.

That's not something TAMO would have bargained for when Messi was signed up for a two-year deal. Messi was supposed to be part of the solution for TAMO: to get its Indian passenger vehicles business to pull up its socks. A global brand ambassador was meant to match the work done on improving the consumer experience. This involved moving on to two new platforms for car making with new power trains and a whole new philosophy. TAMO claims that 'Tiago is on a completely new platform'.

We were focused on three things: great design, driving pleasure, and great connectivity, have worked on the design, making it contemporary and ergonomic, on finding an optimum balance between ride and handling. The car also has two modes that a driver can choose from, a city mode and an eco-mode or a fuel-saving mode, offered first on the Zest. There was also a determined effort to reduce BSR—buzz, squeak, rattle—and provide a good torque curve, something that helps make the car 'sprightly' during city driving. With the Tiago, the company also moved to the new-generation Revotron engines.

Decision time the trajectory that Tiago sales have taken is encouraging. However, the key to turning around operations is creating a family of cars around it, while globally car companies are working on bringing down the number of platforms, TAMO has five. The two older platforms for its cars and SUVs coexist with the two newer ones, and then there is Nano. There are three new launches lined up, which were all exhibited at the Auto Expo 2016 in Delhi.

The Tiago twin, code-named Kite 5 will be a compact sedan. The Tatas already have Zest, a compact sedan and it will be interesting to see how the Tiago twin will be positioned. Then there will be Hexa, the SUV, which is a 'true-blue full-blooded body over frame construction on a completely new platform'; and there is the exciting space of a compact utility vehicle in which the company wants to launch the Nexon.

Conclusions

1. TAMO feel that they have a limited portfolio and expect the volumes to climb gradually with the consistent introduction of new models over the coming years.
2. Meanwhile, the company is trying to ramp up production to cater to demand for the Tiago.
3. Having launched in April, a few months is too short a time to analyse Tiago's success.
4. The Tiago is a game-changing effort towards a robust passenger vehicle business.

Case Questions

1. How TAMO have tried to stand out from its competitors by introducing unique features in Tiago?

2. Discuss the initiatives taken by TAMO to erase its image as fleet cars manufacturer.

Explain the unique vision of TAMO behind creating a family of cars around it, while globally car companies are working on bringing down the number of platforms.

11

RANBAXY—The Indian Pharma Giant

A Case Study in Operations Management and International Marketing

Learning Objectives

To understand the capital structure pattern of Indian pharmaceutical companies with reference to the period before and after TRIPS regime. To understand the relative importance given to the retained earnings, borrowed funds and equity, and preference capital by pharmaceutical companies in the pre- and post-TRIPS regime. To understand the firm-level factors influencing capital structure decisions of pharmaceutical companies in India. To study the relationship of firm-level factors related to inflow of funds and factors related to outflow of funds with the capital structure decisions of Indian pharmaceutical companies. To study the effect of quality of corporate governance on capital structure decisions of Indian pharmaceutical companies. To study the capital structures of sub-groups of pharmaceutical companies based on size, investments in research and development, export sales, and ownership.

Synopsis

Ranbaxy Laboratories Limited was an Indian pharmaceutical company that was incorporated in India in 1961 and remained an entity until 2014. The company went public in 1973. Ownership of Ranbaxy changed twice over the course of its history. In June 2008, Daiichi Sankyo acquired a 34.8% stake in Ranbaxy from the family of CEO and Managing Director

Indian Business Case Studies. Sandeep Pachpande, Asha Pachpande, and J A Kulkarni, Oxford University Press.
© ASM Group of Institutes, Pune, India 2022. DOI: 10.1093/oso/9780192869371.003.0011

Malvinder Mohan Singh for Rs. 10,000 crore (US$2.4 billion) at Rs. 737 per share. In November 2008, Daiichi-Sankyo completed the takeover of the company from the founding Singh family in a deal worth $4.6 billion by acquiring a 63.92% stake in Ranbaxy.

On 7 April 2014, India-based Sun Pharmaceutical and Japan-based Daiichi Sankyo jointly announced the sale of the entire 63.4% share of Ranbaxy from Daiichi Sankyo to Sun Pharmaceutical in a $4 billion all-share deal. Under these agreements, shareholders of Ranbaxy were to receive a 0.8 share of Sun Pharmaceutical for each share of Ranbaxy.

In 2008, Unites States Food and Drugs Authority (USFDA) had originally banned the import of 30 drugs and stopped all future approvals from the pharma giant's troubled facilities, a situation that continues till today. Ranbaxy later shut down one of its facilities (in the US), but has been working with USFDA to rectify the mistakes in the other ones situated in Dewas (Madhya Pradesh) and Paonta Sahib (Himachal Pradesh) in India. This is a story of how the manufacture and distribution of medicines today is such a complex, globalized affair that it is often hard to track where fake or substandard medicines come from and where they go.

In May 2013, Ranbaxy pleaded guilty to felony charges relating to the manufacture and distribution of certain adulterated drugs made at two of Ranbaxy's manufacturing facilities in India, and misrepresenting clinical generic drug data. Ranbaxy pleaded guilty to three felony FDCA counts, and four felony counts of knowingly making materially false statements to the FDA. Included in the adulterated products were antiretroviral (ARV) drugs destined for the treatment of HIV/AIDS in Africa.

Indian Pharmaceutical Industry

The Indian pharmaceutical industry is considered as one of the vibrant industries of the country. The dynamics of the industry changed with the amendment in the Patents Act in 1972 by which the process patents were introduced. The industry prospered since then. The industry continued to depict a vigorous growth in the post-liberalization era. The turnover of the industry went up from approximately USD 1 billion in 1990 to over

USD 20 billion in 2010. The export turnover in the year 2010 was approximately USD 8 billion. The global ranking of the industry was third in terms of volume and fourteenth in terms of value (Department of Pharmaceuticals).

A report by India Brand Equity Foundation on 'Pharmaceuticals' prepared in August 2013 revealed the salient characteristics of Indian pharmaceutical sector.

The Indian pharmaceutical industry is one of the fastest growing industries.

- Its share is equivalent to 1.4% of the global pharmaceutical industry in terms of value and 10% in terms of volume.
- The revenue of Indian pharmaceutical industry is expected to grow at a Compound Annual Growth Rate (CAGR) of 17.8% and would reach USD 36 billion.
- The generics market of India has tremendous prospects and potential. In 2011 it was worth USD 11.3 billion and is expected to reach USD 26.1 billion by 2016.

The sector has attracted 5% of total Foreign Direct Investments (FDIs) in to India from 2000 to 2013.

Ranbaxy Laboratories Ltd

At Ranbaxy Laboratories' Toansa plant in village Rail Majra, just off the dusty industrial hub of Ropar in Punjab's Nawanshahr district, 30 January seemed to be just another day at work. First-shift workers boarded buses outside the factory gate in the early evening while those in the second shift streamed in. The plant's idyllic setting, nestled alongside the Satluj river with the Shivalik range in the backdrop, though, belied a palpable sense of uncertainty among the staffers. Early last month, the US Food and Drug Administration (FDA) notified the company that it was prohibited from manufacturing and distributing active pharmaceutical ingredients (APIs) from the Toansa facility for all FDA-regulated drug products.

Company	Market share (%)	Sales (Rs. Cr) 2016
Sun + Ranbaxy	9.21	9621
Abbott	6.46	4857
Sun Pharma	5.37	4035
Cipla	4.98	3743
Zydus	4.44	3334
Ranbaxy	3.84	2886
GlaxoSmithKline	3.69	2771

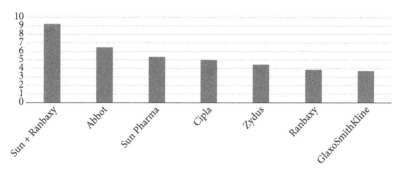

Market share (%)

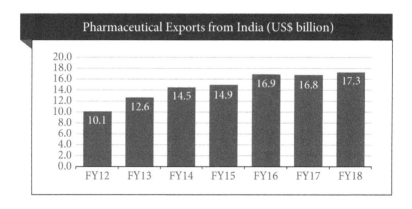

FDA Investigation

'Everybody here knows (of the FDA ban) and is aware of the implications,' a senior supervisory staff at Toansa said. 'We (Ranbaxy Laboratories Ltd) are being targeted. That's the overwhelming sense here. We're not sure how this plays out, nothing has been told to us.'

This underlying sense of pride, albeit badly dented, is unmistakable. Others waiting to board their buses dismissed murmurs of a conspiracy involving sabotage by disgruntled employees in the wake of serious allegations levelled by the FDA about flouting of manufacturing norms at the plant. FDA inspectors found 'too numerous to count' flies in a sample storage room, inadequate control over samples, and non-adherence of procedures in sample analysis.

An internal enquiry initiated by the management of the country's largest pharma firm is still under wraps and queries sent to the Ranbaxy Laboratories' communications team did not elicit a response.

Controversies

The fresh controversy is the last thing the embattled Ranbaxy Laboratory's needs. Before Toansa, its three other plants in India had already been blacklisted by the FDA—its newly commissioned formulation making facility in Mohali (Punjab) was barred in September 2013 after two other key factories, at Paonta Sahib (Himachal Pradesh) and Dewas (Madhya Pradesh), had been put under FDA restrictions in 2008.

There are three key reasons why the Toansa ban is more serious. One, it does not leave even a single Ranbaxy Laboratories facility in India eligible to supply drugs or ingredients to the world's largest pharmaceutical market, the US. Second, while the ban at its Mohali plant was imposed over violation of 'good manufacturing practices', the bulk of the FDA red flags on Toansa allude to much graver allegations of 'data integrity' being compromised. Charges include over-writing of electronic data files and signing of back-dated documents, all of which point to deliberate falsification of data. Ranbaxy Laboratories has been making about 40% of its worldwide revenue of $2.3 billion from the US. In 2012 the last year for which information is available this clocked in at $946 million. So the ban could dent Ranbaxy Laboratories' profits substantially. The Toansa plant is estimated to supply 70–75% of the company's APIs. Even though the series of FDA bans covering all its Indian plants leaves Ranbaxy Laboratories still with Ohm Labs, its US-based formulation plant that can technically continue to make drugs for that market, the American facility was heavily dependent for raw material on the Toansa plant.

While Ohm may already have or can still tie up with a third party to source APIs, profitability will be hit as it would then have to split the revenue.

There could also be fresh trouble brewing as the Indian drug controller, presumably awakened by the FDA actions on Ranbaxy Laboratories, has decided to launch its own inspection of the Toansa facility to assess any possible violations under the Drugs and Cosmetics Act. Drug Controller General of India G.N. Singh is learnt to have issued instructions to his inspectors for an expeditious check of the plant as well as collection of Ranbaxy drug samples from across markets. These would be dispatched for testing in government laboratories.

The company has been guarded in its response. 'This development is clearly unacceptable and appropriate management action will be taken upon completion of the internal investigation,' Arun Sawhney, CEO and managing director of Ranbaxy Laboratories, said in a statement issued by the company in response to Form 483, a form used by the FDA to document and communicate concerns discovered during inspections at the plant in early January 2014. On 24 January, the Gurgaon-based company announced that the FDA had notified the company that it 'is prohibited from manufacturing and distributing APIs from its facility in Toansa, India, for FDA-regulated drug products' and that the 'Toansa facility is now subject to certain terms of a consent decree of permanent injunction entered against Ranbaxy in January 2012'. The company undertook to 'voluntarily suspend shipments of API from this facility to the US market'.

Ranbaxy Laboratories' promise of 'appropriate management action' clearly failed to assuage the markets, with the company's shares tanking, even as brokerages quickly downgraded the stock to 'sell', citing uncertain US business.

Even the most optimistic estimates expect Ranbaxy Laboratories' US business to be 'partially paralyzed' in the near term, putting at risk the expected launch of three 180-day exclusive marketing opportunities in the US this year by the company. The first firm to get FDA permission to sell generics in the US generally gets a lead time of six months before other rivals can start selling the same drug. The three generics expected to be launched this year were versions of Diovan, Nexium, and Valcyte, which fetch over $7 billion in annual sales.

With Ranbaxy Laboratories' credibility already at rock bottom in the eyes of the US regulator, it was expected that it would use a fine toothcomb for the inspection at Toansa. Ranbaxy Laboratories should ideally have been alive to the challenge. The Toansa findings show otherwise.

Then there is the larger issue of how, and by when, Ranbaxy Laboratories manages to stem the problem areas, of which there are several. Though the firm has come a long way from when it started in 1937, with Delhi-based Ranbir Singh and Gurbax Singh getting a license as distributor for a Japanese company Shionogi (the name Ranbaxy Laboratories was a portmanteau of the names of its original owners Ranbir Singh and Gurbaksh Singh), the company's emergence as Indian pharma Bell Weather started with its entry into the US market in 1998. With that came the challenge of increasing levels of scrutiny from global regulatory bodies. The start of systemic issues can be traced back to well before the previous owners of the firm, Malvinder and Shivinder Singh (grandsons of Bhai Mohan Singh, who bought the company in 1952 from cousins Ranbir and Gurbax), sold a controlling stake to the current owners. Japan's Daiichi-Sankyo bought the stake in 2008 for $4.6 billion. The FDA's records suggest that the company acknowledged violations of what are termed as 'current good manufacturing practice or cGMP' regulations for a US-distributed acne drug, Sotret, way back in 2003.

The Damage Revealed

On 13 May last year, the company was forced to plead guilty to felony charges related to drug safety and to pay $500 million in civil and criminal fines under the settlement agreement with the US Department of Justice (DoJ) in the wake of a case against the firm brought by the DoJ built on a vast array of evidence collected by whistle-blower Dinesh Thakur. 'Eight years ago, as the director of Project and Information Management (at Ranbaxy Laboratories), I discovered that the company falsified drug data and systemically violated current good manufacturing practices and good laboratory practices,' Thakur said in the wake of the Ranbaxy settlement.

Thakur maintains that when Ranbaxy failed to correct problems, he alerted healthcare authorities.

The Ranbaxy Laboratories story in recent months has a ring of predictability to it the same sort of question marks on violations of norms, the Ranbaxy management vowing to expeditiously sort out the problem, and the domestic drug regulator promising to investigate the violations. In fact, Sawhney's promise of 'appropriate management action' after the Toansa development is strikingly similar to a detailed communication sent by him to news organizations late last year outlining the road ahead for the company, wherein he had categorically stated that 'the issues that were raised by the US FDA in 2012 have been addressed and we have taken stringent steps. Ranbaxy has strengthened its management, manufacturing and monitoring systems and processes, to ensure quality and compliance in all areas'.

Ranbaxy had also started shipping generic Lipitor, the widely used cholesterol-lowering medicine, from its Mohali plant in April 2012, but six months later, it recalled some of the batches due to the potential presence of glass particles. After that, Ranbaxy had to stop exporting Lipitor from its Mohali plant.

Till the Toansa implosion, Ranbaxy, the setbacks notwithstanding, was actually faring well in the US market. Over the last two years, Ranbaxy had launched several products in the US, including Atorvastatin, Absorica, Desvenlafaxine, and Cevimeline, and continued to market to the US federal government, despite the clampdowns on three of its four plants in India. This was largely on account of the Toansa-Ohm combinations that it was leveraging for the US market. During the period, the company also launched the first new chemical entity, Synriam, for the treatment of malaria in India and has been working towards taking this product to other developing countries.

On the products sold by the company, Sahwney has asserted that 'all Ranbaxy products being supplied in India and globally are safe and efficacious'. Interestingly, this is largely corroborated by the FDA in a note issued on its website after it sent two warning letters and an import alert to Ranbaxy concerning manufacturing issues at the Dewas and Paonta Sahib plants, with regard to about 30-odd different generic drugs that these plants were supplying to the US market. On the specific question of whether Ranbaxy medications were safe to take, the note issued sometime in mid-2009 suggests: 'For consumers currently taking a Ranbaxy product affected by this action, FDA strongly advises these consumers not to interrupt their drug therapy. To date, FDA has no evidence of harm to any patients who have taken drugs made in these two facilities.' To another question, the note says: 'To date, FDA has no evidence of harm to any patients.'

The Repair Job

The periodic disclosures made by Ranbaxy say that the company has been working closely with USFDA for the last three years to re-design its entire operations in the troubled and new production facilities. 'You have a big brother watching over your shoulder', a person close to Ranbaxy said, hinting that USFDA has been monitoring each and every corrective step Ranbaxy has been taking during these years.

The question, though, is of letting down the guard. While time and again its top brass has asserted that Ranbaxy is now a different company and that the entire board has been completely reconstituted from when the FDA violations are believed to have started, the arguments appear watered down in light of the Toansa revelations. It also puts question marks over the investments of $300 million that Ranbaxy Laboratories claims to have made in the last couple of years for upscaling its facilities and employing consultants to impart upgraded skill sets.

Ranbaxy, being the flag bearer of India's emerging pharma industry, has also received the maximum publicity for the violations, though it is not alone in this. India's drugmakers have come under closer scrutiny in the last couple of years with the country emerging as the biggest overseas source of drugs for the US. It is home to more than 150 FDA-approved plants, including facilities run by global players. Pharmaceutical exports from India to the US rose nearly 32% in 2013 to $4.23 billion. India produces nearly 40% of generic drugs and over-the-counter products and 10% of finished dosages used in the US. Reflecting this, in March last year, India allowed the FDA to add 7 drug investigators, bringing its American staff based in India to 19, which includes 10 dedicated specifically to drugs.

An FDA spokesperson, in response to an email query, said the problems encountered by FDA investigators in India are similar to 'those seen around the world in manufacturing'. While some Indian companies operate state-of-the-art facilities and meet GMPs, others do encounter problems and operational challenges, Christopher C Kelly from the FDA spokespersons' office said. 'Staff from the FDA's India office will work with these companies to identify the problems and will take the necessary steps to self-correct,' he said.

Another Indian drugmaker, Strides Arcolab Ltd, had reported a warning letter from the FDA after a June 2013 inspection of a plant of its unit Agila Specialties Pvt Ltd. The production facility of Mumbai-based Wockhardt too had come under the scanner last year, with FDA inspections resulting in bans and import alerts over medicines shipped from India by the company.

Most industry players concede that the spotlight on Indian pharma is here to stay, especially in the wake of the FDA's increasing vigour in safeguarding the interests of the US consumer and the US industry through its modernization programmes. On 12 December 2013, an FDA representative, in a deposition before a Senate subcommittee, stated that the regulator is of the belief that the future of drug manufacturing lies in 'high-technology, computer-controlled production facilities that can rapidly respond to changes in demand and are capable of seamlessly producing a variety of dosages and dosage forms' a yardstick that most Indian drug firms might struggle to meet.

In the submission before the Subcommittee on Energy Policy, Health Care and Entitlements, Janet Woodcock, director, Center for Drug Evaluation and Research, FDA, also stated that the agency's inspection and compliance focus had changed and it had ramped up its inspectorate capability. Woodcock's deposition specifically referred to the use of 'foreign-sourced materials' creating 'vulnerabilities in the US drug supply' and, as a long-term measure, wanting 'to reduce its dependence on imported medicines'.

Conclusions

The larger question still remains. Does Indian pharma need to undertake a trial-by-fire to revamp its manufacturing standards and benchmarks, especially in the wake of apprehensions that the FDA would only sharpen its daggers further and proactive steps from other regulators around the world, including India's own drug controller?

The increased scrutiny could have a bearing on the direction that the Indian pharmaceutical sector goes, as much as in the direction that India's largest drug manufacturer is headed. If the sense of pride evident among the Ranbaxy Laboratories employees waiting for their buses outside the company's Toansa facility is an indication, there is a good chance that the company will bounce back and that should be good news for the Indian drug industry.

This is a story of how the manufacture and distribution of medicines today is such a complex, globalized affair that it is often hard to track where fake or substandard medicines come from and where they go. This is a story of how these medicines could make you ill or even kill you, even if you don't take them.

Case Questions

1. Will there be a drug shortage if products from these two plants are no longer imported into the US and what is FDA doing about it?

2. As a director of the company, what should be your action plan under controversies at Ranbaxy?

3. How the Ranbaxy Laboratories takes the precaution and overcomes these problems?

12

The Two Horse Race

A Case Study in Strategic Leveraging—Value Chain Integration

Learning Objectives

Mahendra & Mahendra tries to produce a new and wider product portfolio at every price to the customer. Focus on customer-centric approach and provide prompt and effective sales service in every city. More focused market survey on rural market and frame a marketing strategy accordingly. Expanded channels of distributions in every city, hence customers get the products at a right time and at a right place. More focus on brand building or the products, hence brand promotion carried out through various media at every place. Designing long-term marketing strategy for easy penetration of products in every place. Adopted the strategies of employee attrition and employee retention, which is helpful for the organizational efficiency.

Synopsis

'We have now become a formidable force in terms of procurement, manufacturer, supplier chain and brand spends', said Dr Pawan Goenka, president, Mahindra & Mahindra (M&M) (auto sector) in respect of integration of sourcing strategies between its farm equipment (tractors) and auto (SUVs and cars)—This a totally new approach of unification/ leveraging two reasonably distinct product lines and naturally therefore raises questions on its feasibility and viability.

Indian Business Case Studies. Sandeep Pachpande, Asha Pachpande, and J A Kulkarni, Oxford University Press.
© ASM Group of Institutes, Pune, India 2022. DOI: 10.1093/oso/9780192869371.003.0012

Two years ago, a team led by Bishwambhar Mishra, chief executive of M&M's tractor and farm mechanization division, was scouting around for a location in the south to set up a manufacturing plant. A group member suggested using the site of the auto factory in Zaheerabad in Andhra Pradesh to make tractors as well.

The unit, set up in 1985, makes three- and four-wheel transportation vehicles like the Gio and the Alfa, Navistar light commercial vehicles and M&M's best-selling utility vehicle (UV), the Bolero. In a few months, the first tractor will roll out from that plant.

For the first time in the history of M&M, UVs and tractors will be produced in one plant (the company does make tractors and UVs in Kandivali in Mumbai, but in two independent plants). 'We are utilising the location to create a robust supplier park-which is justified now because of increased volumes-to benefit both the businesses,' says Pravin Shah, chief executive of M&M's automotive division.

The blueprint for Zaheerabad was one of the early initiatives by M&M towards an unlikely integration of two pretty diverse businesses. True, they both run on wheels and are powered by engines, but tractors and automobiles are dissimilar lines addressing different sets of customers, which, in turn, call for different positioning and go-to-market strategies.

At the back end, though, it's a different story, with synergies available for the taking across multiple fronts, from procurement to inventory management. The benefits are wide-ranging, including more efficient management of working capital and logistics improvements in quality (lighter tractors, for instance) and even gains in talent management, as two teams collapse into each other.

Introduction

Mahindra & Mahindra Limited (M&M) is an Indian multinational vehicle manufacturing corporation headquartered in Mumbai, Maharashtra, India. It was established in 1945 as Muhammad & Mahindra and later renamed as Mahindra and Mahindra. It is one of the largest vehicle manufacturers by production in India and the largest manufacturer of tractors in the world. It is a part of the Mahindra Group, an Indian conglomerate. It was ranked 17th on a list of top companies in India by Fortune India 500 in 2018. Its major competitors in the Indian market include Maruti Suzuki and Tata Motors Ltd.

Mahindra began manufacturing tractors for the Indian market during the early 1960s. It is the top tractor company in the world (by volume) with annual sales totalling more than 200,000 tractors. Since its inception, the company has sold over 2.1 million tractors. M&M's farm equipment division (Mahindra Tractors) has over 1,000 dealers servicing approximately 1.45 million customers.

The farm equipment division was established in 1963 in the form of a joint venture with International Harvester Inc., and Voltas Limited, and christened as the International Tractor Company of India (ITCI). In 1977, ITCI merged with M&M and became its tractor division. After M&M's organizational restructuring in 1994, this division was re-christened to the farm equipment sector division. Today M&M is the largest manufacturer of tractors in India. It designs, develops, manufactures, and markets tractors as well as implements which are used in conjunction with tractors.

Background of M&M Ltd

M&M, the flagship company of the USD 3 billion Mahindra Group, was set up in 1945 to make general-purpose UVs for the Indian market. It soon branched out into manufacturing agricultural tractors and LCV and later expanded its operations from automobiles and tractors to other sectors. The company has recently started a new division, Mahindra Systems and Automotive Technologies (MSAT) in order to focus on developing components and to offer engineering services. M&M has two main operating divisions—automotive division and farm equipment division. The company entered into collaboration with Willys Overland Corporation (now part of the Daimler Chrysler group) to import and assemble the Willys Jeep for the Indian market. Thereafter, in 1965 the company started producing LCV. It went on to develop its manufacturing technology to indigenously produce vehicles within a short time of signing the collaboration agreement with Willys. Today, the automotive division of M&M manufactures and markets MUV, LCV and three-wheelers.

The Mahindra Automotive and Farm Equipment Sectors (AFS) is one of the largest contributors to the Mahindra Group revenue and includes 27 businesses, 18 subsidiaries, and 9 companies.

The automotive business accounts for about 48% of India's UV market share and is the number two CV player in India. The business has a presence in almost every segment of the automobile industry with SUVs, luxury UVs, sedans, pick-ups, light, medium, and heavy commercial vehicles to three-wheelers. Their customer base spans rural and urban India.

The farm equipment department also provides irrigation, fertilization, seeds through varied agriculture, and allied businesses.

Thinking about M&M Ltd

It all began in April 2010 when M&M, the only manufacturer in the world that makes both farm equipment and passenger vehicles under one company, decided to explore the potential gains of having both manufacturing lines under one roof.

The M&M brass, including then Anand Mahindra (vice-chairman and MD), Rajeev Dubey, president (HR), Bharat Doshi (Group CFO), and Pawan Goenka, president (auto sector) and now president (auto and farm equipment) got into a huddle to see if an integration was indeed worth the effort.

Anand Mahindra felt the time had come for the next big step-up. Both businesses have had long solo rides. M&M's first UV was made in 1947, and tractor production began in the early 1960s. Anand Mahindra, who on 30 May was designated as chairman and managing director of M&M, recalls when he joined in 1991 the company was steeped in a license raj culture.

Over the years, M&M had transformed into the world's largest tractor company by volume, and into India's number one maker of UVs that span the price spectrum and are sold in continents from South America to Australia. 'Today, the need of the hour in increasingly competitive global markets is to become ruthlessly efficient in driving down costs and deriving synergies,' says Mahindra.

Agrees Vijay Govindarajan, professor at Tuck School of Business at Dartmouth College: 'M&M has global ambitions. You need size and scale to compete globally against automobile giants like Toyota, General Motors, Ford and agricultural tractor powerhouse John Deere. A combined sector gives M&M the global clout,' says the author of books like 'Reverse Innovation' and 'The Other Side of Innovation'.

The Integration Work

Such a global vision called for a new structure that retained the market focus—with two CEOs for two sectors—but created a third head who combines the R&D and purchase functions of the two sectors, paving the way for synergies in these high-spend functions. Goenka, as president of both the auto and farm sectors, now oversees the CEOs, ensuring that synergies are driven right from the top.

'We have now become a formidable force when it comes to procurement, manufacturing, supply chain, brand spends, among other benefits,' adds Goenka. The more visible—although not necessarily most useful—signs of the integration are at the front end. For instance, tractor dealers in rural markets—some 1,100 of such outlets—also sell transportation three- and four-wheelers.

Yet, the integration efforts are more pronounced at the back end in areas like sourcing, engineering, and product development. As Goenka says, expectations of an auto consumer are different from that of a tractor buyer, so integrating the front end is not an imperative. Jagdish Khattar, former MD of Maruti, points out that M&M's auto and tractor integration works as a big tool in sourcing and HR retention. 'The integration will largely benefit the business, but the front end should be kept independent,' adds the founder of Carnation Auto, a multi-brand auto solutions network.

Benefits through Integration

Economies of scale began to kick in on the increased volumes of the combined entity—450,000 units of auto (UVs, cars, trucks, and transportation vehicles) and 250,000 units of tractors in 2011–2012—on various fronts like working capital management, logistics, and just-in-time inventory.

As Pravin Shah, chief executive (automotive division), puts it a game plan of 700,000 is far better than one of 450,000. Both the auto and tractors source material and components as one entity, thereby deriving more bargaining power.

The benefits for both sectors are mutual, though tractors would seem to be gaining more. For instance, automotive has a robust product development process called the 'gateway' process: a product or a process will not move to the next 'gate'—or stage—unless it meets certain parameters of quality and performance The tractor sector has absorbed the gateway process and two new product platforms are benefiting from it (more synergies). Automotive too stands to gain from the robust quality processes in tractors, which helped reduce defects per 1,000 by around a fifth.

On the HR front, the assimilation throws up possibilities for career rotation and succession planning. 'Movement of talent has become easier and roles have been enhanced,' explains Rajeev Dubey, president (Group HR), 'Earlier, there was no commonality, so it was difficult to move people from one sector to another.'

The Challenges

There were apprehensions to deal with. For instance, the farm equipment guys felt that auto would play a role of big brother. After all, auto is larger and growing faster, though margins as compared to farm equipment. Also, hierarchical conflicts, particularly on the technical front-auto employees, would see themselves as 'higher-tech' workers than those in tractors were inevitable. Goenka spent six months explaining the benefits of the exercise to employees in farm equipment via town-hall meetings and discussions.

'We spoke one language, portrayed one market scenario,' says Rajan Wadhera, as the change is difficult, the endeavour has been to pick out best practices (from both sectors) and deploy them without affecting cultural sentiments. Putting all managers and workers into one melting pot has helped M&M identify more candidates for critical positions.

'We have identified 73% successors for critical positions as against 55% before the sectors were integrated,' explains Rajeshwar Tripathi, chief people officer automotive and farm equipment sectors. Two years after the process began, Mahindra and Goenka can ill-afford to rest on their oars. Synergies in areas like the field force and manufacturing have yet to be fully exploited and that is an imperative if the integration has to qualify as a resounding success. Also, talent retention is one of the biggest challenges M&M faces, and rivals point out that the integration may be the culprit. Goenka acknowledges the challenge of assimilation and compares the integration to a big-ticket acquisition in which two organizations with different cultures, expectations, and approaches to business come together.

Tractors and automotive may have been two big pieces of one legal entity, but culturally they were different businesses, he stresses. Yet, the end game in any big acquisition is to make one plus one equal three, and it's no different within M&M as Mahindra and Goenka pull out all stops to squeeze out more from the sum of the company's two workhorses.

The Growth Drivers

There are several key drivers that have affected the automobile industry in India. These include:

Government Regulations

The automobile industry in India has received extensive government support and this has encouraged a lot of foreign direct investment in the industry. The government permits 100% foreign direct investment in this industry and it is fully de-licensed making it easy for investors to penetrate it and set up shop in India. Additionally, there are also tax incentives and investors can actually export the automobiles for free.

Low Car Penetration and Rising Family Income

India has about 120 vehicles (all segments including 19 cars per 1000) on every 1000 people right now, which is expected to rise to almost 300 in the next 10 years. Around 60% of the mobility demand in India is served by public transportation modes like buses and metros and non-motorized transport modes (walking and cycling). India's per capita income grew at a pace of 8.6% to Rs. 1,12,835 (1375 Euro) during FY18 from Rs. 1,03,870 (1265 Euro) in FY17. The growing domestic income is to make motor vehicles more affordable for local consumers.

Young Population

India is one of the youngest countries in the world with more than 50% of the population is below the age of 25 years and more than 65% is below the age of 35%. A young population may lead to higher personal vehicle ownership.

Greater Availability of Cheaper and Easier Finance

All nationalized and scheduled banks offer loans for the purchase of new vehicles at very low interest rates. In India nearly 70–75% of the new vehicle purchases are done by using bank loans. This indicates that Indian auto industry is unique in the way vehicles are purchased by consumers.

Research and Development

There have been many research and development initiatives, both private and governmental. These are aimed at improving the automobile industry in India. The government started the Automotive Component Manufacturers Association of India (ACMA) which is an apex body that deals with the automobile industry in India. This body looks into matters such as upgrading of technology in the industry, collecting information on industrial events and trends as well as disseminating this information to relevant stakeholders. The body does this through research and also promotes trade in both domestic and foreign circles. On their part, private investors have also set up research and development initiatives within their companies. For instance, the M&M research centre for electric vehicles in order to enhance their services in India.

Stable Economy

Many experts predict that the future of the automobile industry in India is bright. However, this is subject to the economic stability of the country and currency inflation rates. Economic stability and low inflation will increase incomes for the majority of Indians and raise the domestic consumption of automobiles in the country.

Financial Status of M&M Products

Financial Status of Automobile Segments of M&M

S. No	TYPE	PUBLIC
1	Products	**Automobiles**, commercial vehicles, two-wheelers
2	**Revenue**	₹105,806 crores (US$15 billion) (2019)
3	Operating income	₹8,870 crores (US$1.2 billion) (2019)
4	Net income	₹6,016 crores (US$840 million) (2019)

Financial Status of Farm Equipment Segments of M&M

S.NO	TYPE	FY2017	FY2018	FY2019
1	Revenue (Rs.bn)	136	162	181
2	Growth (%)	23	19	12
3	EBITDA (Rs.bn)	26	33	36
4	EBITDA Margin (%)	19	20	20

Market Share of M&M Vehicles

The Market Share of Passenger Vehicles of M&M

Company	Maruti Suzuki	Hyundai Motors	M &M	TATA Motors	Honda Motors	Others
Market Share (%)	49.8	16.3	7.56	6.39	5.17	14.6

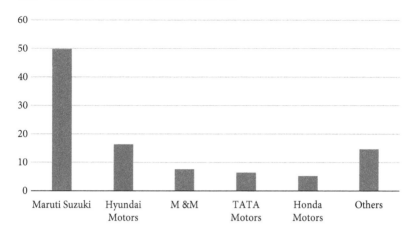

Market Share (%)

The Market Share of Commercial Vehicles of M&M

Company Name	Apr–Mar F.Y 2018	Market share (%)	Apr-Mar F.Y 2019	Market share
TATA Motors	376456	43.93	447,323	44.41
M & M	216,803	25.30	248,601	24.68
Ashok Leyland	158,612	18.51	185,065	18.37
VECV-Eicher	55,872	6.52	61,732	6.13

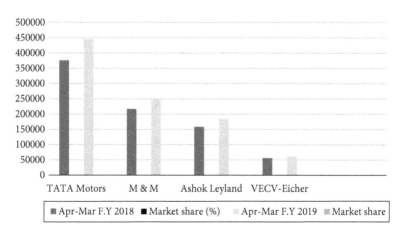

Market share of C V

The Market Share of Farm Equipment (Tractor) Division of M&M

OEMs	Market share in FY'18 (%)	Market share in FY'19 (%)
M&M (with PTL)	41.6	40.2
TAFE (with Eicher Motors)	18.6	18.4
Escorts Ltd	10.7	11.8
Sonalika	11.8	12.2
Others (John Deere, New Holland etc)	17.3	17.5

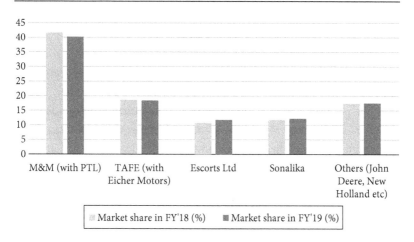

Market share of Farm Equip. division

Future Plans

Going forward, the company's growth is expected to be driven by the farm equipment division in the backdrop of greater focus on the farm sector by the Government, improved agriculture infrastructure like irrigation and easier availability of rural credit. M&M with its range of tractors across all segments is well placed to keep pace with the market. The emerging second-hand tractor market provides an interesting opportunity for the company. The farm equipment division has started an initiative 'Mahindra Vishwas' that aims at organizing the second-hand tractor market. This initiative will help generate additional new tractor sales as well as expand the second-hand tractor market. Under the automotive division, the Logan, expected to be introduced in 2007, will give M&M a world-class product in the mid-size passenger car segment, which is expected to be one of the fastest-growing segments in the Indian passenger car industry. With MUV gaining popularity, Scorpio's sales will continue to grow. With the company entering new export markets, it is expected to double its volume of exports within a year. This increase in volume will be driven by entry into selected large potential markets like Russia and launch of new products like the Scorpio Pick-ups.

Conclusions

M&M motors, the only manufacturer in the world that makes both farm equipment and passenger vehicles under one company, decided to explore the potential gains of having both manufacturing lines under one roof. It has a good market share in vehicle segment as well as in farm equipment segment. The company is offering good services, which is reflected on the satisfaction of the customer.

The majority of the customer are satisfied with the design as well as after-sales services provided by the company. If the company were identifying the pitfalls in their products and undertake remedial measures thus it will lead to more good word of mouth publicity.

Case Questions

1. According to global practices in strategic business management/ leveraging and integration of similar activities such as product and processes is considered as essential for generating synergic benefits on productivity, costs, and timelines (delivery)—M&M's strategy to integrate two reasonably dissimilar products, process, and market major divisions into one common 'Strategically integrated business is like the two horse race'.

Comment on the likely hurdles in implementation of such a strategy. (M&M has successfully run the two businesses separately for nearly two decades establishing market leadership.)

2. How do you see the problems as expressed in the case study for talent management and flexibility in terms of job rotations when the executives have negative perceptions on the integration efforts? Do you have any success stories of similar strategies elsewhere in the industrial scenario?

3. What are the precautions that the two horse strategy needs to adopt as a fallback in case of serious hurdles in its successful implementation?

13

'Beating a Dead Horse'

A Case Study: Revival of Air India—The Forgotten Maharaja

Learning Objectives

Air India is the giant public sectors undertaking having many rewards and achievements to its credit. However for past few years the company is in news for its vulnerable condition and financial distress. The present study is intended to understand the case history of Air India, the performance trend of the company. The primary objectives of the case study include the objective to understand the achievements and failures faced by the giant, explore the causes of its downfall and financial distress, and finally the measures suggested by the experts as well the measures implemented by the company to overcome the crisis.

Synopsis

Despite popular airlines suffering through the crippling debts, it is said that the market will boom in the coming years. The major problems suffered by the aviation industry lies in the fact that they are chasing to acquire market share and not profits.

The airline has suffered years together because of its status as a public limited organization as the case of majority of the public sector undertakings in India. Lack of business attitude and aptitude dig the grave of the public sector undertaking.

Indian Business Case Studies. Sandeep Pachpande, Asha Pachpande, and J A Kulkarni, Oxford University Press.
© ASM Group of Institutes, Pune, India 2022. DOI: 10.1093/oso/9780192869371.003.0013

The Case Study

Over the period of 75 years of our independence, the nation has achieved the remarkable economic growth through planned industrial development. There are many public sector as well as private sector companies who led years together in this development. Air India is one of the giant public sectors undertaking having many rewards and achievements to its credit.

However the scenario for Air India has been disappointing. Everyone is curious to understand how an 88 years age old giant organization, one-time market leader which ruled the aviation industry decades together becomes so fragile that experts and industry stalwarts are not coming to any conclusive decision in favour of this giant: The Air India.

The Evolution of Air India

Air India was founded by J.R.D Tata, the then business tycoon and an Indian aviator, in April 1932. It was named as Tata Air Services initially then changed as Tata Airlines. It became public limited company on 29 July 1946 and then named as Air India. After Independence, the Indian government has acquired major stake in the organization, 49% in 1948 and subsequently the majority stake in 1953. The company was renamed as Air India International Limited and the domestic aviation business was transferred to Indian Airlines. Over the period the company had many achievements to its credit. By inducting its first Boeing 707–420, in 1932, it became the first Asian airline who inducted jet aircraft in its fleet. It became the world's all jet airline in 1962. Air India One is the Air India aircraft used for carrying prime minister, president, or vice president. The industry giant became 27th member of Star Alliance in 2014. It also won many prestigious awards till July 2019. Over 60 international destinations are served by Air India across four continents.

The Present Scenario

The Directorate General of Civil Aviation said that from January 2018 to September 2018, domestic Indian airlines flew more than 10 crore passengers, showing a growth of 20.94%, the highest in the world. However though there found a huge growth in the business, it is not reflected through the financial achievements of the sector; the sector is struggling and trying to sustain in the dynamic world. Along with the shutdown of Jet Airways and the Kingfisher scam, Air India too is in very dicey situation. The government-owned airline suffered a loss of 8,556 crores of rupees in financial year 2018–2019. More than 15 top executives have left the aviation sector, Indigo with its largest market share also suffering from the technical glitches.

Reasons for Downfall of Air India

The crucial part in construction of a building or any civil construction is the construction of its pillars. The pillars that hold the skyscrapers matter the most. In business world the decision-making authorities are the pillars, who creates a strong foundation for the business to grow and sustain in the prevailing situation. There are many factors contributing to the downfall of the organization like:

1. Wrong investment decisions:
Purchase of 90 aircraft/airbuses by Air India and Indian Airlines put together in 2006–2007: Without conducting a market survey for passenger requirements these investments were done. According to a CAG report, five Boeing 777s and five Boeing 737 were kept on ground from 2007 to 2009 resulting into a loss of Rs. 840 crores.

More than 150 foreign pilots were hired at a very high cost to fly these aircrafts. Instead of outright purchase, like other airlines the government would have leased the plains.

Moreover under the bilateral agreement government gave the profitable international routes to private players outside India.

2. Loss making international operations:
In most of the international routes the company was even unable to recover its costs. The flights to North America and Europe were resulted into a loss of Rs 2,323.76 crores in 2015–2016. Because of the completion from other airlines, the company had 77% occupancy on Delhi-New York—Delhi route.

3. Mismanagement of manpower:

The employee strength was double than what is required as per the industry standard. There found to be excess manpower in admin and finance departments as the employee union has indicated. Moreover there was underutilization of pilots and cabin crew. For instance for wide-body and narrow-body aircraft the requirement of pilots is 291 and 554 respectively whereas in 2015–2016 the company has 86 pilots in excess.

4. Non-availability of proper aircraft:

The mismatch in the demand and availability of aircraft has been observed by the auditor, there was over-provisioning of wide-body aircraft whereas it didn't have the required number of narrow-body aircraft. This was brought to the notice of the management of the airline. The airline took three years to float a global tender which jeopardized the plan of reducing maintenance costs.

5. Less income in passenger revenue:

The airline lost revenue due to its own inefficiency like lack of aircraft availability, faulty deployment, low utilization of human resources, and lack of ancillary revenue.

6. High finance cost:

As per the annual reports the financial cost of the airlines in 2018–2019 and 2017–2018 was 18.47% and 19.45% of the operating revenue respectively.

7. Continuous losses since 2006–2007:

The airline has incurred huge losses decades together, which pile up the loss burden year after year. Air India showed a net loss of Rs 8,400 crore in 2018–2019. The operating loss of Rs 491 crore till 2 July 2019.

8. High debt burden:

Air India's total debt stands at Rs 58,000 crore, along with a cumulative loss of Rs 70,000 crore.

9. Merging Air India and Indian Airlines:
The two airlines were merged in 2007 to gain the synergy effect, however, the results were disastrous and the losses mounted.

10. A turnaround plan that did not work:
In 2011, the UPA-II government decided to pump in an equity of Rs 48,212 crore for a period of 20 years starting 2011–2012 and ending in 2031–2032 to stop Air India from bleeding.

Air India was expected to show positive earnings from the financial year and a cash surplus from 2017 onwards. The opposite happened. Air India's inability to service the annual interest payments led to the losses amounting to Rs 52,000 crore this year. In the meantime, the national carrier had exhausted the Rs 25,000 crore committed under the turnaround plan.

11. Leasing aircraft, incurring losses:
The Central Bureau of Investigation (CBI) has raised charges of irregular leasing of aircraft by Air India without due consideration, a proper route study, and marketing-pricing strategy.

'It was alleged that the aircraft were leased even while aircraft acquisition programme was going on.' According to CAG, the estimated losses from leasing of aircraft stood at Rs 405.8 crore between March 2011 and May 2014.

12. Selling aircraft for a lower price:
According to the CAG report, in March 20017, Air India incurred a loss of more than Rs 671 crore by selling five Boeing 777–200 long-range aircraft to Etihad below cost price.

Air India sold these five Boeing to Gulf carrier Etihad for USD 336.5 million, which comes to roughly USD 67.3 million per plane.

According to CAG, the aircraft were sold at a price lower than the indicative market price of USD 86–92 million per aircraft obtained from two parties, M/s AVITAS and M/s ASCENT.

The losses mount when one adds the interest paid on loans to procure these aircraft which stands at Rs 324.6 crore.

The Measures Implemented by the Airline and by the Government

Air India, the crowned prince of the Indian aviation market, the government-protected airline company, is again entering the bidding market, after the failed attempts in 2018. However, in this fresh bid, the Indian government softened the terms to make sure that the debt-laden Air India is sold to private buyers easily.

As per the management discussion analysis as part of financial report 2018–2019, the airline has taken the following steps for turnaround:

1. Rationalization of Human Resources.
2. Restructuring of city offices in India and abroad.
3. Close monitoring of overtime allowances.
4. Focus on sale of business class seats.
5. Reducing cost of capital.
6. Rationalizing commission to agents.
7. Rationalization of certain loss-making routes.
8. Induction of brand new fleet on several domestic and international routes by increasing passenger appal.
9. Phasing out old fleet and consequent reduction in maintenance cost.
10. Reduction of contractual employment and outsourced agencies.
11. Increase in passenger, cargo, excess baggage revenue through aggressive sales and marketing strategy.
12. Up-gradation of FFP and introduction of several marketing initiatives including companion.
13. Free schemes, apex fare, GOI packages, preferred agents partnership, promotion of web bookings, and other promotional schemes like AI Holidays, etc.
14. Reduction in cabin crew hotel cost by shifting to lower priced hotels.

Conclusions

Indian Aviation industry plays an integral part in the development of the economy as a whole and is one of the major contributors to increase the employment level in the country. Air transport is an important factor of transport infrastructure of a country, and has a significant contribution in the development process by creating employment opportunities, improving the productivity, and more efficient transportation of goods and services. It also enhances business growth, tourism, and trade across the economy. With a long existence in the field, Air India would have been the flagship organization for aviation industry. Air India is an example of ineffective and irrational management.

'If one does not know to which port one is sailing, no wind is favourable.' It is the apt saying for the age-old giant. The airline has suffered years together because of its status as a public limited organization as the case of majority of the public sector undertakings in India. Lack of business attitude and aptitude dig the grave of the public sector undertaking.

In business every day is a new day with new challenges and new ways of facing these challenges. Air India needs to learn the new strategies that Indigo has successfully implemented. The low-cost model in every operation of the airline helped Indigo sustain in the market. It is always better to learn from one's mistakes and others success, in order to retain oneself in the competition.

Despite popular airlines suffering through the crippling debts, it is said that the market will boom in the coming years. The major problems suffered by the aviation industry lies in the fact that they are chasing to acquire market share and not profits.

Case Questions

1. What has really gone wrong in the management of Air India even once known as national carrier?

2. Is there a deliberate ignorance or strategic drift in the overall execution plans for profitable operations of Air India?

3. How the turnaround of the big giant will take place?

14

Business Sustainability and Indian Aviation Sector

A Case Study Focusing on Low-cost Carriers in Indian Aviation

Learning Objectives

To understand the aviation industry sector working with special emphasis on Low Cost Carriers (LCC). To understand what business strategies lead to successful businesses. To be able to interpret numerical and visual market data. To develop analytical skills for judging success and losses in business. To differentiate between profit-making and loss-making strategies.

Synopsis

IndiGo Airlines, the country's largest low-cost carrier, announced a five-fold increase in net profit to Rs 787 crores for 2012–2013 straight for the fifth year, contrarily, rivals Jet Airways and SpiceJet together made a loss of over Rs 671 crores in the same year, Kingfisher Airlines went belly up, state-owned Air India, despite the infusion of fresh equity from the government and a slight improvement in performance, struggled and the industry lost Rs 46,000 crores in the five years. The huge profit happened in spite of adverse market conditions; rising fuel costs (up 13%), weakened rupee (7%), and domestic traffic down (3.4%) in 2012 over the previous year. How did such huge profits accrue? This case analyses the secret ingredients that continue to make Indigo the most successful aviation and, will it sustain its momentum?

Indian Business Case Studies. Sandeep Pachpande, Asha Pachpande, and J A Kulkarni, Oxford University Press.
© ASM Group of Institutes, Pune, India 2022. DOI: 10.1093/oso/9780192869371.003.0014

Company Background

IndiGo is an Indian airline company headquartered in Gurgaon, India. It is a low cost carrier (LCC) and the largest airline in India with a market share of 30.3% as of September 2013. IndiGo is one of the fastest-growing LCCs in the world. With its fleet of 72 new Airbus A320 aircraft, the airline offers 447 daily flights connecting to 35 destinations.

Indian Aviation Industry—Current Scenario

Aviation sector not only brings immense benefits to communities and economies around the globe, but also is a key catalyst of economic growth, social development, and tourism. It facilitates connectivity and access to international markets. Air transport currently supports 56.6 million jobs and accounts for over USD 2.2 trillion of the global gross domestic product (GDP). India is the ninth largest aviation market handling 121 million domestic and 41 million international passengers. Today, more than 85 international airlines operate in India and 5 Indian carriers connect over 40 countries.

Business Model of LCC or LFC

An LCC or Low Cost Carrier follows an airline business model that uses the latest technology, from aircraft through to systems, operating at high utilization, to eliminate those costs that do not add to the guest experience.

This enables an LCC to bring the same high level of safety to air travel, but with the lowest fares to the routes or markets that it serves. These are usually markets that have traditionally suffered from high prices and reduced service enabling more people to fly that otherwise would not have done. LCCs democratize air travel in this way.

Fuel is the airlines' second largest cost (about 10 to 12% of total expenses), and travel-agent commissions are third (about 6%). Commission costs, as a percent of total costs, have recently been declining, as more

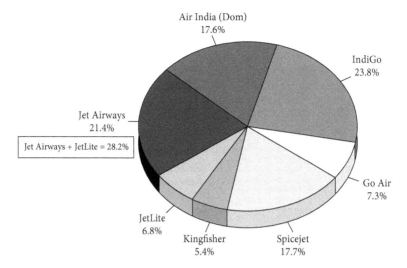

Figure 14.1 Market share of scheduled domestic airlines

sales are now made directly to the customer through electronic commerce. Another rapidly rising cost has been airport landing fees and terminal rents.

Government policy measures such as lower cost airport infrastructure, lower taxes on aviation fuel, and a move away from looking at airlines as a luxury business could help decrease the cost of airline operations and thus help the airlines either lower prices or have higher realizations at the current price levels.

The following Table 14.1 lays out the business model of an LCC.

As can be seen in the pie chart, Indigo has the largest market share followed by Jet Airways and Spice Jet.

The above Table 14.2 shows how Indigo optimized its variables for the highest profits at a time when all other airlines sustained losses.

Indigo's Counterintuitive Strategies

The airline has adopted a counterintuitive strategy of adding new aircrafts and expanding capacity amid the slowdown, which seems to be paying off.

Table 14.1 Business model of an LLC

Low Cost Carrier (LCC) Business Model	
Simple Product	• Catering on demand for extra payment
	• Planes with narrow seating and only a single class
	• No seat assignment
	• No frequent flyer programmes
Positioning	• Non-business passengers, especially leisure traffic and price-conscious business passengers
	• Short-haul point to point traffic with high frequencies
	• Aggressive marketing
	• Secondary airports
	• Competition with all transport carriers
Low Operating Costs	• Low wages
	• Low airport fees
	• Low costs for maintenance, cockpit training and standby crews due to homogeneous fleet
	• High resources productivity
	• Short ground waits due to simple boarding processes
	• No air freight, no hub services, short cleaning times, and high percentage of online sales

Source: http://businesstoday.intoday.in

Table 14.2 Comparative indicators for different domestic airlines

	Net Revenue	Profit/ (Loss)	Aircrafts	Destinations	Flight per day	Load Factor	Market Share
Indigo	9,458	787	70	34	447	80.8	29.1
SpiceJet	5,714.55	-191	55	54	370	74.31	17.2
Jet Airways	17,070	-480	120	75	620	78.8	25.1
Air India	16,130	-5,198	108	95	400	64	19.9

Some of its strategic initiatives are:

- Punctuality records are the best and it ensures customer loyalty. The airline charges more or is at par with a full-service airline in some of the busiest routes. Thus, even though its cost per available seat is one of the lowest, its revenue per seat is nearly at par, which explains the sharp difference in operating profit.
- Deft route planning—provide more capacity on select routes, rather than spread itself thinly over several destinations. Indigo has a fleet of 70 aircraft, yet it flies to only 29 domestic and 4 international destinations. IndiGo was able to increase the passenger load factor by six percentage points, and increase its domestic market share of the domestic skies from 22% in 2012 March to 28% in 2013.
- 'Power by hour' agreements with vendors under which it pays for every hour the aircraft flies; in return, the vendors provide full spares and replacements whenever they are required. Hence more 'air' time for aircraft and no inventory maintenance costs along with prevention of airline from shocks (like a sudden problem in the engine requiring replacement).
- IndiGo's employee-aircraft ratio has improved from around 120 two years ago to 100–102 now. In striking contrast, Jet Airways has a ratio of 130, while Air India's ratio is 262.
- Tough turnaround target time—31 mins. Hence the plane is kept airborne for 12 hours a day.
- Fleet consists of one kind of aircraft: the Airbus A-320. As a result, it is required to deal with one set of pilots, spares, and engines. This simplifies the process of running the airline and also keeps costs on a tight leash.
- Reduction of fuel burnout after flight has landed, hence saving 50% of the operational cost.
- Maintaining healthy cash flow positions with no working capital loans.
- Lighter in-flight magazines.
- New planes to be added to the fleet; A-320 Neos which are 15% more fuel-efficient.
- Every plane in the fleet is fitted with ACARS. Before every departure, an automatic message is triggered from aircraft to control centre and

the departure time is recorded immediately. Similarly, the moment the flight lands an automatic message is triggered from aircraft to control centre. These timings are recorded in 'real time' and without human intervention.

Recent Issues

IndiGo, the fastest growing airline in India, could face some headwinds going forward as other airlines become more competitive. Jet Airways is expected to place an order for 50 A320 Neos which will be deployed for LCC operations under its subsidiary, JetKonnect. Air India has already firmed up plans for a sort of hybrid LCC operation, where it has decided to lease 19 Airbus 320 aircraft with an all-economy seating. Then, AirAsia, the ultra-low-cost airline from Malaysia, is likely to begin operations before the year comes to an end and another South East Asian LCC is also expected to come down to India.

No wonder then that the LCC space, where IndiGo has more than a fourth of the market, is expected to get extremely competitive in the next 1–2 years. So, the airline needs to deepen its focus on the domestic business. However Aditya Ghosh, the current CEO of Indigo Airlines, seems to defer and shows no plans to rope in a strategic partner or go for an IPO. His outlook for the current fiscal FY-14 was to increase fleet by adding roughly a new aircraft every five weeks.

IndiGo is expected to focus on the introduction of unbundled products which enable it to offer more of the features of a full-service airline—and generate ancillary revenue—without changing the underlying business model. This could include for example lounge access, priority boarding, customized meals, and loyalty programme membership, all on a user-pays basis. Rather than a hybrid airline, IndiGo appears to be pitching itself as a 'corporate LCC'.

Why Jet Failed to 'Konnect'?

The no-frills brand scored poorly on perception, performance, popularity, and profit.

Jet Airways is going back to its roots after five years of flirting with a no-frills brand. The airline has promised a full service two-class cabin offering across its entire fleet by the year-end-a move triggered by weak performance and cold customer response to its no-frills brand Konnect.

Jet Airways launched Konnect in May 2009 'to meet the needs of the low fare segment and complement its full service product'. It began by offering no-frills service on three planes and a handful of routes. In 2012, even the subsidiary JetLite's service was rebranded as Konnect. Today it covers about 60% of Jet Airways' domestic flights and all of JetLite-operated flights. However, the Konnect brand has failed to earn both popularity and profit.

While Jet Airways lost domestic market share as it cut capacity, data provided by the Directorate General of Civil Aviation show that the airline has been carrying fewer passengers per flight than its rivals. In 2013, Jet Airways reported a load factor of 71.5%. Load factor is an indicator of occupancy and Jet's loads were lower than GoAir, IndiGo, SpiceJet and only marginally higher than Air India.

Even in the first seven months of 2014, Jet Airways' load factors are amongst the lowest in the industry and the achieved loads are far lower than what's required to break even on domestic routes. Jet Airways' domestic operations contributed about 45% of its total revenue and nearly 70% of its pre-tax loss on a standalone basis in FY 2014.

In FY 2014, Jet posted a record Rs 4,129 crores loss due to one-off maintenance expenses and Rs 700 crores on account of the negative net worth of its subsidiary JetLite.

The Konnect brand has had to grapple with perception issues. Last week, Jet Chairman Naresh Goyal acknowledged that the airline had confused customers with two brands and announced that the airline will streamline domestic operations, create a strong, uniform Jet Airways master brand, and improve its product and service offering.

Jet executives admit running two brands on domestic routes with a Boeing 737 fleet having various seat configurations has been a challenge as it gave little operational flexibility and impacted brand consistency. Along with brand overhaul, Jet Airways is also reconfiguring its fleet to a standard 168 seat configuration (12 business class and 156 economy class) and is restructuring its frequent flyer programme to woo customers.

While IndiGo has been very creative with its advertising and marketing focusing on punctuality and service reliability, Jet Konnect created a perception that it is only a re-branded version of JetLite or Air Sahara, a Jet executive remarked.

'Operating Boeing 737 with various configurations did not give us flexibility. These have 8–16 business class seats and the balance economy seats. From an operational point of view when an aircraft develops snag, another one was put in service. That allowed us to maintain our on-time performance but often it impacted brand consistency and confused customers,' the executive said. With a standard 168 seat configuration, the airline will not face the problem.

The changes in the frequent flyer miles programme will also benefit customers. Until now, miles were awarded to passengers based on distance flown. For shorter routes of 100–200 miles, the award was restricted to 100–200 mileage points. Further, there is a disparity between miles offered on Jet Airways and Jet Konnect flights (Konnect flights only earn 75% of miles earned on Jet Airways flights).

After the change, a passenger will earn a minimum 500 miles even for short distance flights. Additionally when Konnect brand gets phased out, passengers will earn miles uniformly on all flights. Jet executives also argue that the cost of a switch over to a full-service model across the entire network would be small but the service itself can be a key differentiator. 'In the current environment, cost of fuel, maintenance, lease, airport charges are high and largely similar for all airlines. The cost of delivering additional services, miles etc is minimal,' he said. Also, while the airline will stop charging for food, it can and will still continue to charge fees for other services—date changes, extra luggage, cabin upgrades, seat selection, and so on. 'I think the main trigger for Jet's brand overhaul could have been the start of the Tata-Singapore Airlines venture, Vistara, which seems to have a precise strategy in mind. I am sure Etihad was a participant in the decision. From Etihad's point of view, I would think it would want to have an airline in its simplest form possible—lean and mean, as they say. That would be a good base from which to build. Combining the two operations should increase efficiency as long as they are willing to eliminate redundancies in personnel and infrastructure,' said Jet Airways' former CEO Steve Forte.

The Future Uncertainty

With the government allowing more overseas investment in Indian airlines, IndiGo faces competition from foreign airlines that could bring in higher operating standards as well as higher ultimate cost of travel to the passenger.

Airlines in India need to fly domestically for five years before they are permitted to fly internationally, and IndiGo is using this opportunity to fly some routes once a day that already have very heavy competition. This international initiative is also going through a testing phase.

The Indian Aviation Industry is on the verge of tremendous growth and is showing great potential with regards to the future. IndiGo is well-positioned to take full advantage of this scenario and is likely to emerge as a major player in the aviation industry. With other competitors making alterations to their business model and gearing up for the new fiscal, it remains to be seen if IndiGo can sustain its momentum.

As far as Jet is concerned, brand experts say the overhaul was inevitable as Konnect did not stand for anything except a watered-down version of Jet. 'The most common error companies make while launching a low-cost variant is to position it as a cheaper version of the premium brand. That should never be the case as a lower priced product has the opportunity of reaching out to a new segment. That opportunity would be lost as nobody wants to buy a brand that is perceived cheap. Jet Konnect should have been positioned differently, perhaps as a younger, vibrant brand,' said brand expert Alok Nanda.

Saurabh Parmar, founder and CEO of Brandlogist, says the problem with Jet is that over the years it has had multiple brands like Jet, JetLite, JetKonnect, and Konnect Select. But the airline failed to innovate and worse, created a huge confusion. *Now, that's a sure recipe for failure.*

Conclusions

IndiGo has indeed been very successful in making a strategy mix for its success, taking advantage of the current market scenario, and developing a unique LCC product that took advantage of the market opportunities and government policy and support. Its strategic management both within and outside of the company was smart and well thought out; this led to their success while others failed.

Case Questions

1. Under present-day fight for sustainability and severe competition, can the low-cost airlines continue to prosper (even survive—as Jet has announced to dissolve Jet Lite and Jet connect routes and perhaps more to follow); could there be a sustainable business model for low-cost airlines? Can they maintain their market share and competitive advantage?

2. What are the strategic differences between low-cost airlines (Fringe Airlines) operating with fair amount of business confidence in countries abroad and Indian aviation industry?

3. What could be the recommendations for a sustainable business model low-cost airlines survival and growth in India?

15

Can SpiceJet Be Resurrected?

A Case Study in Business Turbulence

Learning Objectives

To understand the cyclical nature of SpiceJet's product cycle. To analyse the success strategy and losses of SpiceJet. To be able to apply strategic management principles to SpiceJet. To evaluate business strategies that lead to the success of a business. To analyse business strategies that lead to failure.

Synopsis

From a healthy Rs 800 crores in 2010, created over a five-year period to a loss of Rs 1003 crores in four years by 2014, SpiceJet did an inverted V within less than a decade, nine years to be precise. This roller coaster ride downwards occurred in the absence of its' creator Mr Ajay Singh. SpiceJet seems to flourish whenever he is at the helm of its operations. This case study documents the ups and downs of the carrier and the challenge Mr Ajay Singh has taken up to turn around the commuter airline.

Introduction

The first thing that you see when you walk into the Gurgaon office of SpiceJet is a three-foot T20 cricket trophy won by the employees' cricket team. Incidentally, the man at the helm of SpiceJet, Ajay Singh was the cricket captain of St Columba's School, Delhi (where actor Shah Rukh

Indian Business Case Studies. Sandeep Pachpande, Asha Pachpande, and J A Kulkarni, Oxford University Press.
© ASM Group of Institutes, Pune, India 2022. DOI: 10.1093/oso/9780192869371.003.0015

Khan kept wickets). Back then, there was no T20 format. Since Singh's cricketing days at school, when he was a number four batsman, the game has become faster, pitches have changed dramatically and the competition got harder.

Things have changed for SpiceJet too. When Singh walked away from SpiceJet in 2010, the brand he co-created in 2005 had Rs 800 crores in the bank. Now, when he is back as the promoter, the firm is in an air pocket of deep losses and has Rs 5 crores in cash.

The past year or so has been particularly traumatic for SpiceJet. Its market share fell from 20.9% in July 2014 to 10.4% in December 2014. The airline, which made a net profit of Rs 67 crore in 2009–2010, made a loss of Rs 1003 crore in 2013–2014. 'It is not going to be an easy job turning Spice Jet around. It is not a healthy market place anymore,' says Praveen Paul, a Bangalore based aviation consultant.

Taking Guard

Ajay Singh's priority is to clear all the dues, of around Rs 1400 crore. He has been doing that since he took over SpiceJet, on 24 February, announcing that it has cleared its major outstanding dues related to Income Tax (TDS) payments. It had earlier this month also cleared all service tax dues and employee salaries and the dues on plane rentals to lessors for six of its Boeing aircraft. Of the Rs 1500 crore which has been committed by a group of 'blue chip' investors including Singh, Rs 500 crore has already been infused into the airline.

Since he took over, flight control directly reports to Singh and he gets messages on his phone about flight delays. He wants to make the airline more punctual. 'The majority of the people just want to travel from one place to the other and be on time on a neat and safe plane,' says Singh. SpiceJet now has a fleet of 17 Boeings and 15 Bombardiers and COO Sanjiv Kapoor says, 'We will grow our international network, but with a focus on flights that are no longer than four hours flying time to maximise efficiency. We have withdrawn from several international routes in the past year (which) were unprofitable, and we have added capacity to the more profitable routes.'

The other important task at hand is to rebuild the confidence of the staff. 'We have cleared all salary dues till date. In fact, February salaries have already been paid on February 28. We witnessed a natural attrition which we did not refill because of the decrease in fleet size,' says SpiceJet CFO Kiran Koteshwar.

SpiceJet's Timeline

1993–1996: ModiLuft, run by SK Modi and Lufthansa.

May 2005: Ajay Singh and Bhupendra Kansagra join hands. Modi Luft becomes SpiceJet.

August 2008: Wilbur Ross, the distressed assets buyer, acquires a controlling stake in SpiceJet.

Mid-2010: Kalanithi Maran acquires 38.7% stake. Ajay Singh quits board.

March 2012: Q4 losses mount to Rs 249 crore.

August 2013: CEO Neil Mills quits.

2014: Days of struggle—with fleet reduction and flight cancellations rumours of a shutdown.

30 January 2015: SpiceJet board approves Rs 1500 crore share sale.

24 February 2015: Ajay Singh is back as promoter.

Bouncers and Brickbats

With the new management in place, SpiceJet is under greater scrutiny—from both the aviation industry and customers. The airline's move to reintroduce flash sales has reignited the debate if such moves hurt the industry. 'Flash sales are designed to get rid of seats that are expected to otherwise go empty, at rates that provide a return that is greater than the marginal cost of flying the passenger in that seat,' says Kapoor.

Ankur Bhatia, executive director, Bird Group which provides ground handling services to SpiceJet echoes the same opinion. 'Globally, every airline does flash sales.' Customers too are keenly looking for changes.

Sinju Venugopal, an HR consultant and a frequent flyer of the Hyderabad-Cochin sector, says, 'Spice Jet nowadays doesn't provide meals in their flight. During morning and night flights, it is a difficult proposition.' Recently, even Omar Abdullah, former chief minister of Jammu and Kashmir tweeted: 'Due to technical reasons fly spice jet isn't able to provide food for sale on flights. Please sort out these technical reasons quickly guys.' Singh admits that this is a vendor issue. But he insists that priorities lie elsewhere, like flying on time.

There is a lot of expectation on Singh, who is known to be a good boss across the industry. Many staffers had quit SpiceJet during the crisis last year and were looking for jobs elsewhere. Air Costa was one of their options. R. Promod, who was involved with hiring at Air Costa at the time, says, that they had given offer letters to many of them who came for the job interview. 'As soon as the news came in that Ajay Singh is coming back, they all went back to Spice Jet,' says Promod, who is now vice president, Airport Services at Fly Easy, a regional airline.

SpiceJet has gone through a near-death experience and Ajay Singh seems to have given it a kiss of life. The question is can he nurture it back to good health? The answer, perhaps, lies in the past.

SpiceJet's origins date back to February 1984, when it was incorporated as Genius Leasing Finance and Investment Company Limited and it entered into aviation, when industrialist SK Modi tied up with German Airlines Lufthansa. This was one of India's first post-de-regulation airlines, ModiLuft. Flying to five destinations, it operated between 1993 and 1996.

Cornell University alumnus Ajay Singh first came to the scene in 2004 when London-based businessman Bhupendra Kansagra came to him with an idea of revamping the defunct ModiLuft. Singh already had a reputation as a turnaround man. Having worked on the board of Delhi Transport Corporation (DTC) and as an advisor to the Telecom Ministry (the rank of a joint secretary), he knew how to revive albatrosses.

When Singh joined DTC in the mid-1990s, it was in a state of despair with a few hundred buses. By the time he left, after two and a half years, the corporation had a fleet of around 6,000 buses. He was also appointed by the Information and Broadcasting Ministry to revamp the national broadcaster Doordarshan. These experiences are set to weigh in as he tries to turn around SpiceJet.

'The plan (for Spice Jet) started around October 2004 and I announced that we will start operations in May 2005,' recalls Singh. People around him said it was impossible. But using the same license of ModiLuft to fly, with three leased aircraft, and Rs 10 crores of investment from Singh, SpiceJet took off on 23 May 2005. The first ball hit by Singh was a masterstroke. The tickets which were sold at a base price of Rs 99 were a sellout and the initial flights had a passenger load of almost 90%.

'I saw the effects of tariff reduction in the telecom sector. I was sure that this low cost model can be adapted to the aviation sector,' says Singh.

Five things you may not know about Ajay Singh.

1. He has tried his hand at flying, but failed 'horribly'.
2. He was associated with the Department of Telecom at the time of mobile telephony revolution in India.
3. He has worked with the Delhi Transport Corporation.
4. He was the student of the year in his last year of school. The next year, Shah Rukh Khan bagged the honour.
5. At school, he captained cricket and hockey teams.

The Declaration

By 2008, the honeymoon period was over. All airlines in the country started bleeding due to rising fuel costs. 'Spice Jet was also losing money, but not as bad as other airlines. We needed fresh equity,' says Singh who had only a minor stake in the company but was heading the airline's day to day operations.

SpiceJet got a breather when maverick investor Wilbur Ross injected $68 million in the country's second largest low-cost carrier in mid-2008. In 2010, Kalanithi Maran of Sun Group and Kal Airways (controlled by Maran) bought a 38.66% stake and gradually they increased the stake. 'The management control went to Mr Maran and I sold my stake in the company,' says Singh.

That was the beginning of the not so good times. 'Marans treated it as their family business, not as a public company,' says an industry observer who did not wish to be quoted. The airline's losses, in the fourth quarter of 2011–2012, quadrupled to Rs 249 crore compared to the corresponding quarter of the previous financial year.

'In aviation business, there has to be laser sharp focus. The introduction of Bombardier planes proved costly,' says Captain G.R. Gopinath, the founder of Air Deccan. All over the world, low-cost airlines run with one type of aircraft. SpiceJet under Marans brought in Bombardier Q 400s in addition to the existing Boeing 737-900 ERs and 800s. This increased costs as there had to be separate teams for different aircraft.

More pains followed. The airline had to pay more than a year of tax dues worth Rs 380 crore between August and November. SpiceJet began returning planes. This led to fleet reduction which the company called as 'fleet restructuring', which resulted in flight cancellations. SpiceJet was spiralling out of control.

Six Ajay Singh's mantras for SpiceJet's turnaround.

1. 'It's not rocket science, just keep it simple!'
2. 'Fly fewer stations with higher frequency'.
3. 'Build as much excitement over ancillary products'.
4. 'Up the reliability and performance of the fleet'.
5. 'Fly on time'.
6. 'Make the unit cost lowest possible'.

Outcome—The Second Innings

The path for Singh's re-entry was paved in the first week of December 2014. A video conference connected Chennai to the Gurgaon office of SpiceJet in Udyog Vihar. Maran and Singh were face to face. Maran wanted to exit the business. In January 2015, the SpiceJet board approved the Rs 1,500 crore stake sale and after the approval from Competition Commission of India (CCI), Ajay Singh made a full circle on 24 February 2015.

Conclusions

Almost everyone in the industry drew comparisons with Kingfisher Airlines, which bit the dust not so long ago. SpiceJet had looked down the abyss, but managed to stay afloat. 'Ajay Singh's proximity to the government also helped. Ajay Singh saw the reality, but Mallya didn't believe till the end that something has gone wrong with the airline,' says Jitender Bhargava, former executive director, Air India and the author of 'The Descent of Air India'.

But Chief Operating Officer (COO) Sanjiv Kapoor clarified to the public that this was not a 'bailout'. 'There was no funding of any kind involved from the government or taxpayer funds; it was simply a few weeks of credit based on standard commercial terms,' Kapoor explains in the in-flight magazine 'Spice Route' given to flyers.

Singh expects to turn around the airline by March 2016. For now, like any good middle-order batsman, he seems to be focusing on the job at hand, ball by ball. The guy, who started selling cheap plane tickets ten years ago, is just settling down. Casually dressed in his red SpiceJet t-shirt and blue jeans, he looks at ease seated in his office at Udyog Vihar. But, the airline itself has to do a lot more. As Bhargava says, 'it is time for them to hop, step and jump.'

Case Questions

1. Outline the fluctuations in the two decades life of SpiceJet.

2. 'A business is synonymous with it's leader', explain this statement in relation to Mr Ajay Singh. Analyse the business strategies used by Mr Singh for SpiceJet success.

3. What were the reasons for the SpiceJet debacle, what strategies would you suggest to avoid it.

Do you think the Indian market conditions support new businesses? Would government policy or the absence of it better to support such businesses?

16

The Death of a Dream

A Case Study on Rise and Fall of Nokia in India

Learning Objectives

Nokia was one of the first handset companies to enter the Indian market in the early 1990s and the brand almost became generic to cell phones. Its hold on the Indian market was far stronger than in the international market. Adding to this is the fact that the Indian mobile phone market grew at a scorching pace in the early 1990s. This case focuses on how Nokia started one of its largest manufacturing facilities in India. However, along with the rest of the world, Nokia lost its leadership position in India, unable to capitalize on the smartphone trend.

Synopsis

Once a showpiece of foreign investment, the factory at Sriperumbudur, about 45 km from Chennai, now looks like a ghost entity. For the around 30,000 workers, 31 October 2014 will forever be Black Friday as Nokia officially shutdowns its plant in the state, nine years after it entered India. Nokia's closure will be the first major wind up by a multinational after the new government took charge in May. Established in 2006 over a 200-acre site, Nokia wheeled out the 'Made for India' 1100 model and then slowly ramped up production to make Chennai its single largest unit for handsets globally. Nokia and its suppliers had invested over Rs 1,800 crore in their facilities.

Nokia started operations at Sriperumbudur plant near here—the second biggest facility by any global firm—in 2006 after Korean auto

Indian Business Case Studies. Sandeep Pachpande, Asha Pachpande, and J A Kulkarni, Oxford University Press.
© ASM Group of Institutes, Pune, India 2022. DOI: 10.1093/oso/9780192869371.003.0016

major Hyundai's came up with its plant in the late 1990s. After inking the agreement with the Tamil Nadu government in 2004, Nokia began operations at the facility. It directly employed 8,000 people and another 25,000 were associated indirectly with the firm when the facility was operating in full swing. The facility was producing some of the basic GSM handsets. It was serving the local market, besides exports. However, its decision to sell off the handset business to Microsoft Corp in a $7.5-billion deal forced it to keep the factory out of the agreement due to a tax dispute with Indian authorities. The plant's success attracted attention.

Nokia Company

Nokia is a leader in the fields of network infrastructure, location-based technologies and advanced technologies. Headquartered in Espoo, Finland, and with operations around the world, Nokia invests in the technologies of the future. Nokia has three strong businesses:

1. Nokia networks, network infrastructure business;
2. The plant location intelligence business;
3. Nokia technologies, which is focused on technology development and intellectual property rights activities.

Through these businesses, it has a global presence, employing around 57,000 people. Nokia is also a major investor in R&D, with investment through the three businesses amounting to more than EUR 2.5 billion in 2013. Until recently, Nokia also was a key participant in the mobile devices market through its Devices and Services business. In September 2013, Nokia announced an agreement with Microsoft whereby it would sell substantially all of its Devices and Services business to Microsoft. The transaction was completed on 25 April 2014.

Background History of Nokia

Nokia has a long history of successful change and innovation, adapting to shifts in markets and technologies. From its humble beginning with one paper mill, the company has participated in many sectors over time: cables, paper products, tires, rubber boots, consumer and industrial electronics, plastics, chemicals, telecommunications infrastructure, and more. Most recently, Nokia has been best known for its revolutionary wireless communication technologies, which have connected billions of people through networks and mobile phones.

Nokia's history dates back to 1865, when mining engineer Fredrik Idestam set up his first wood pulp mill at the Tammerkoski Rapids in Southwestern Finland. A few years later he opened a second mill on the banks of the Nokianvirta river, inspiring him to name his company Nokia Ab in 1871.

In 1967, it took its current form as Nokia Corporation as a result of the merger of Idestam's Nokia AB, Finnish Rubber Works, a manufacturer of rubber boots, tires, and other rubber products founded in 1898, and Finnish Cable Works Ltd., a manufacturer of telephone and power cables founded in 1912. The new Nokia Corporation had five businesses: rubber, cable, forestry, electronics, and power generation.

Nokia first entered the telecommunications equipment market in 1960 when an electronics department was established at Finnish Cable Works to concentrate on the production of radio-transmission equipment. Regulatory and technological reforms have played a role in our success. Deregulation of the European telecommunications industries since the late 1980s has stimulated competition and boosted customer demand.

In 1982, when Nokia introduced the first fully digital local telephone exchange in Europe, and, in the same year, the world's first car phone for the Nordic Mobile Telephone analogue standard. The technological breakthrough of GSM, which made more efficient use of frequencies and had greater capacity in addition to high-quality sound, was followed by the European resolution in 1987 to adopt GSM as the European digital standard by 1 July 1991. The first GSM call was made with a Nokia phone over the Nokia-built network of a Finnish operator called Radiolinja in 1991, and in the same year, Nokia won contracts to supply GSM networks in other European countries.

In the early 1990s, it made a strategic decision to make telecommunications its core business, with the goal of establishing leadership in every major global market. Basic industry and non-telecommunications operations—including paper, personal computer, rubber, foot-wear, chemicals, power plant, cable, aluminium, and television businesses—were divested between 1989 and 1996. By 1998, Nokia was the world leader in mobile phones, a position it enjoyed for more than a decade.

In 2006, Nokia, which had already been investing in its mapping capabilities for many years, acquired Gate5, a mapping software specialist, and then in 2008 NAVTEQ, the US-based maker of digital mapping and navigational software. Today, Nokia offers leading location services through the HERE business and brand, launched in 2012.

In 2007, Nokia combined its telecoms infrastructure operations with those of Siemens to form a joint venture named Nokia Siemens Networks (NSN). NSN has become a leading global provider of telecommunications infrastructure, with a focus on offering innovative mobile broadband technology and services.

In 2011, Nokia joined forces with Microsoft to strengthen its position in the highly competitive smartphone market. Nokia adopted the Windows phone operating system for smart devices and through their strategic partnership Nokia and Microsoft set about establishing an alternative ecosystem to rival IOS and Android. In 2011, Nokia also started to make a number of changes to its operations and company culture that would in the course of the next two years lead to shortened product development times, improved product quality, and better responsiveness to market demand.

In 2013, Nokia moved to reinvent itself with two transformative transactions. The first was the purchase of Siemens' stake in NSN, which was nearing the end of a deep restructuring and remarkable transformation. The second was the announcement of the sale of substantially all of Nokia's Devices and Services business to Microsoft. The Microsoft transaction was originally announced on 3 September 2013 and was completed on 25 April 2014.

Following the closing of the transaction, Nokia announced its new vision and strategy, building on its three strong businesses: Nokia Networks, HERE, and Nokia Technologies.

History of Nokia Operations in India

1 December 2004

Nokia announces its decision to set up a plant in India. Till then, it used to import all handsets sold in India from China.

6 April 2005

Nokia signs MoU with Tamil Nadu to set up the plant in Sriperumbudur Special Economic Zone (SEZ). It invited seven of its ecosystem partners to invest. Nokia initially committed to an investment of about $150 million for five years. Its cumulative investment grew up to $300 million.

2 January 2006

Sriperumbudur plant starts commercial production of handsets with 550 people. Nokia first equipment vendor to manufacture both mobile devices and network infrastructure equipment in India.

11 March 2006

Sriperumbudur facility inaugurated by Finland Prime Minister. Factory starts with low- and mid-range GSM handsets, which includes the Nokia 1100 model. Jorma Ollila, chairman and CEO, was also present. Sale crosses one million mark in the same month.

June 2009

Sriperumbdur factory has edged past China as a unit-wise volume producer of Nokia cell phones and becomes Nokia's largest cell phone manufacturing facility in the world.

1 May 2010

Nokia crosses 250 million handset mark and starts exports to North America and Europe.

5 May 2011

Production crosses 500 million handsets, marking a significant milestone for Nokia's manufacturing operations in India and globally. The milestone was achieved in five years of its operations, marking Chennai's ramp-up among the fastest globally.

End of March 2014

Plant's cumulative production was 800 million handsets. Exports worth more than $2 billion a year. Nokia India's overall turnover totalled Rs 151,000 crore between 2005/06 and 2011/12.

In its prime days, the Sriperumbudur plant was one of its biggest handset manufacturing facilities, producing over three lakh handsets a day. At its peak, the Nokia factory employed around 8,000 people directly and another 25,000 indirectly. But ever since its tussle with the income tax authorities for non-payment of dues of Rs 21,000-crore to the centre and Rs 2,400-crore to the state, and the Microsoft take-over deal of Nokia's handset business, the company has been pruning its workforce. Microsoft made it absolutely clear it was not interested in fighting the tax department in India and hence decided to leave the Chennai plant out of the deal.

Overview

Nokia Structure: Structure Optimized for Growth and Innovation

Nokia has a simple and clear operational governance model, designed to facilitate innovation and growth. Its three businesses report to the Nokia President and Chief Executive Officer, Rajeev Suri, who has full accountability for the performance of the company. HERE and Nokia Technologies each have a single leader reporting to him. To ensure efficiency and simplicity, Mr Suri assumes direct control of the Nokia Networks business and key Nokia Networks leaders report to him.

The primary operative decision-making body for the company is the Nokia Group Leadership Team. The Group Leadership Team is responsible for group level matters, including the company strategy and overall business portfolio.

Go, Get Nokia

It was all very different on 1 December 2004, when Nokia first announced its decision to set up a plant in India. Till then, it used to import all handsets sold in India from China. 'India was doing about a million phones a month at the time,' says a former Nokia executive who does not want to be named. Nokia wondered how it could make this a six to seven million a month market.

The answer was local manufacturing. An Indian facility meant lower logistics costs, less time to hit the market, more flexibility. No longer would executives have to get in touch with the China factories for small design changes which took nearly three weeks to be executed and products shipped. When Nokia revealed it was scouting for a manufacturing destination in India, many state governments—Haryana, Andhra Pradesh, Uttarakhand, Karnataka, and Maharashtra, along with Tamil Nadu—competed to woo it.

In 2004, when Nokia first announced that it was scouting for a manufacturing plant in India, Tamil Nadu moved the fastest and won the race. 'Quick access to an international airport was an important condition since phones are low value, high volume products,' he says. 'Chennai airport was only 33 km away.' Uttarakhand and Andhra Pradesh promised to build international airports, but no one in Nokia believed either would be able to do so quickly. (Hyderabad did not have its new airport then; that happened only in 2008.)

Tamil Nadu bureaucrats claim that, 'They made a good presentation.'

'We understand the mind of investors,' 'Never say "No problem" to them.'

'It had everybody's blessings,' the former Nokia executive says.

Nokia signed a memorandum of understanding with the Tamil Nadu government on 6 April 2005, to set up the plant in the Sriperumbudur SEZ. It invited seven of its ecosystem partners to invest. Production started in 2006.

Tax Tussle

8 January 2013: Income Tax Department inspects the Chennai factory.

21 March 2013: IT Department issues a Rs 2080 crore tax demand, later rectifies to Rs 2,649 crore on Nokia. Later matter moved to Court.

February 2014: Tamil Nadu sends Rs 2,400 crore sales tax notice.

April 2014: Nokia completes the sale of Devices and Services business to Microsoft globally, excluding Chennai factory which was frozen by IT Department. Company announces VRS to employees.

6 October 2014: Company says that from 1 November 2014, it will suspend operations at Sriperumbdur as Microsoft is ending its sourcing agreement with Nokia.

In a separate tax case, the Supreme Court had ordered Nokia India on 14 March to give a Rs 3,500 crore guarantee before it transfers the plant to Microsoft. As a consequence, Nokia entered into a transitional services agreement with Microsoft to address their immediate production needs and keep the factory operational. 'Unfortunately, the continuing asset freeze imposed by the tax department prevented Nokia from exploring potential opportunities for the transfer of the factory to a successor to support the long term viability of the established, fully functional electronics manufacturing ecosystem.'

What Triggered to Shutdown?

The mothballed Sriperumbudur plant of Nokia, once the world's single largest mobile phone-making unit, may be sold in parts. The Finnish company has appointed Hilco, a global leader in handling distressed investment and assets, to take over the machinery and hard utilities. Hilco officials undertook a due diligence at factory last Friday. Nokia suspended production at the facility from 1 November. 'They did a complete assessment of the plant and its machinery,' sources said. While the value of machinery lying idle inside the plant is not known, sources said that it could be worth close to 54 million euros, including hard utilities like continuous process unit, generators, capacitors, chilling plant and others. 'The decision to sell the plant in parts was taken by Nokia as take over the plant by a buyer appears remote due to obsolete machinery and technology. Today, nobody makes Nokia phones and therefore the scope for someone to buy the plant appears remote,' sources said. The factory, assets of which were frozen by the tax authorities, will move to Central Board of Direct Taxes (CBDT) as Nokia had only an operating license after the Tahsildar of Kancheepuram attached it due to non-payment of taxes, as ordered by CBDT. For any transactions at the plant, the courts must defreeze the assets. In a global transaction, Nokia announced its sale of handset business, including its Sriperumbudur plant, to Microsoft for 5.4 billion euros last year. The deal deadline of 31 March was extended to April 2014. Several cases and tax disputes surfaced after the deal with Microsoft was announced, and the Sriperumbudur plant was left out of the deal. Nokia ran the plant as a contract manufacturer for Microsoft for one year.

Tax authorities say Nokia violated several tax laws, including transfer pricing laws and permanent establishment liability, which if proven will result in a tax charge in excess of Rs 21,000 crore on the Finnish company. 'As of now, the tax authorities have issued demands for Rs 3,080 crore. Of this, Nokia was directed to pay Rs 500 crore by the Delhi high court which the company has paid,' sources said.

With Nokia shutting down the plant, its key component supplier Foxconn too has announced the suspension of production from 24 December. Nokia's decision to suspend production in India left many wondering what triggered the move, as the company had earlier said its factory in Sriperumbudur was among its most productive globally. While the tax holiday for the factory coming to an end might be a factor, many say the business model of Microsoft (which acquired Nokia's handset division last year), as well as freebies offered by the Vietnamese government, might also have played a role.

Responding to a detailed questionnaire sent by Business Standard, Microsoft said, 'As part of Microsoft's mobile devices strategy announced in July, we are in the process of realigning our manufacturing operations. As such, we have determined we no longer require the manufacturing services of the Chennai factory and have informed Nokia we will end our agreement on October 31.' The US firm said it would focus on the mass smartphone market. 'There is no future if you don't have share.

We will build scale and share. We will unlock more products in the $100–200 price range to address the mass market,' Chakrapani Gollapali, country general manager (consumer channels group) at Microsoft Corporation India, had said earlier. The company's 'affordable' smartphones would hit the market in three–four months, he added. Currently, the company has one product in this category—the Nokia Lumia 520.

HR Issues at Nokia

Chennai: The plant's shutdown has rendered over 8,000 workers jobless.

Workers fret over the future, over 30,000 people were affected. With Nokia deciding to suspend operations, trade unions as well as political parties have asked the government to take over the factory to protect the livelihood of thousands of workers.

The general secretary of Centre of Trade Unions (CITU) and a sitting member of the Tamil Nadu Legislative Assembly said the CITU has asked the state and Centre governments to take over the factory. Nokia India Employees Union, which claims to have the backing of workers at the factory, is backed by CITU. Earlier, in order to protect the interests of workers at Neyveli Lignite Corporation, a Centre government-run company, the Tamil Nadu government had come forward to acquire a 5% stake in the company, which the Centre was planning to dilute to outsiders. Similarly, the state government or the Centre should take over the Sriperumbudur factory, taking thousands of Nokia workers' livelihoods into consideration, Soundararajan said. He said the factory can manufacture mobile phones, laptops, and set-up boxes. So, if the government can convince customers such as Microsoft and others, orders will start flowing to the factory, he noted. The major reason given by Nokia for suspending operations at the Sriperumbudur plant is a lack of orders, especially after Microsoft decided to stop sourcing from the plant.

'We can confirm that constructive discussions with union representatives and the labour commissioner have resulted in an agreement on a financial package for Chennai factory personnel,' the spokesperson said in a statement a day after a tripartite meeting here between company officials, union members, and the top labour officer. At the time of closing down the operations, about 1,100 employees were working in the plant, including 900 on the assembly lines.

With the month-long voluntary retirement scheme (VRS) announced by Nokia India coming to an end on Wednesday, 15 May 2014, 5,000 employees of the mobile handset facility in Sriperumbudur near here have opted for it. Another 400 are expected to opt for VRS. This could be one of the largest VRS offered by any company in India in recent times, said sources. The factory directly employs 6,700. A little over 60% are women. Nokia India said, 'While we set no target for the VRS in terms of employees, 5,000 have opted for it.' Workers who had not opted for VRS asked, 'With the balance 1,700 workers, how will the factory be run?' The company said, 'Nokia intends to respect commitments under the services contract.' Workers said many had queued at the office to opt for VRS on Wednesday. The union has demanded a withdrawal of VRS.

On those opting for VRS, sources said workers in the facility for five years or more (some have been for eight) would get compensation that would include 15-month salary (each year of experience would be three months). Those with less than five years would be compensated on a similar basis. A worker would get Rs 1 lakh each as compensation and double the daily salary for the earned leave surrendered. To support those that have taken up VRS, the company has introduced a bridging initiative. It is offering banking consultancy services and employment outlook training. It is introducing initiatives under the bridge.

These include working with experts to identify new employment areas, developing suitable training and skilling employees, conducting awareness sessions to share information on 30 skill development modules and employment outlook training schemes across sectors.

The company said, 'The training programs will be held over a period at 40 locations in Tamil Nadu, including Chennai.' It would certify employees on the skills learnt, invite potential employers to facilitate placements, and give limited grants to support entrepreneurial or academic ambitions of those who have worked for six years or more.

Around 72% of the Nokia plant's employees were women. Indeed, the job with Nokia transformed the lives of many of the women, most of who were from poor families—young high school pass outs taking up their first jobs. 'We realized the importance of Nokia not only from the narrow angle of employment generation but also through the change it brought about in the employees' lives.'

Nokia India has said it would suspend operations from 1 November. Around 6,000 jobs, direct plus indirect, are at stake.

'We are worried of the situation. The management is not giving us proper reply on the fate of the factory or the job security of the workers,' said Kumar. There are around 8,000 employees under direct employment in the facility whereas around 21,000 are employed indirectly for the company in Sriperumbudur.

Meanwhile, sources inform that almost all the over 700 trainees are resigning from the company, accepting the retirement option offered by the company. According to the union sources, the package offered by the company for trainees includes three months' gross salary along with Rs 2 lakh as compensation. Nokia employees at Sriperumbudur to get severance package of Rs 7.5 lakh each.

A final settlement was reached for over 900 workers still employed at Nokia's phone manufacturing unit in Sriperumbudur on Thursday, a day before the official closure of the plant. The deal arrived at gives the staff a sum slightly higher than the amount of Rs 6 lakh announced through a VRS.

A tripartite meeting between the Nokia India Thozhilalar Sangam—the workers' union, the company management and the labour commissioner's office concluded on Thursday, bringing about an amicable financial settlement for the 912 employees and 28 clerical and contract staff remaining in the Nokia unit.

'The plant has been operating at Sriperumbudur near Chennai since 2005 and enjoying several benefits offered by the state government since then. However, without intimating the labour the State or Central government, the company was sold to Microsoft,' said Soundararajan, who is also a sitting MLA.

Conclusions

1. Nokia's ultimate fall can be put down to internal politics.
2. In short, Nokia people weakened Nokia people and thus made the company increasingly vulnerable to competitive forces.
3. Nokia's culture of status has led to an atmosphere of shared fear which influenced how employees were interacting with each other.
4. The human factor was added to economic and structural factors and together they have generated a state of 'temporal myopia' that hindered Nokia's ability to innovate.
5. Employees stated that top managers and directors were no longer abiding by Nokia's core values of respect, challenge, achievement, and renewal.
6. This study points out the paramount importance of shared emotions among employees and their powerful impact on the company's competitiveness.

Case Questions

1. Did politicians cock a snook at Nokia staff? Why job security of about 30,000 employees (directly and indirectly employed) was simply not taken care of by central and state government?

2. Why Nokia could not look at possibilities of taking the case to international courts?

3. Why Nokia Tamil Nadu factory could not be saved, though government had option of running under public-private partnership?

4. The rise and fall of Nokia's Sriperumbudur plant raises larger questions about India's attractiveness—or otherwise—as a manufacturing destination?

17

The 'Walkart' of India

A Case Study on Walmart-Flipkart Merger

Synopsis

US retail giant Walmart has signed a definitive agreement to acquire a 77% stake in India's largest e-commerce marketplace Flipkart with an investment of around $16 billion, making it the largest transaction in the history of the online retail space globally.

The deal, which wiped away $10 billion of Walmart's market capitalization as investors reacted negatively in early morning trade on the New York Stock Exchange, stands out for several exits. The biggest was Sachin Bansal selling his entire 5.96% stake for $1.23 billion and parting ways with Flipkart that he had founded in 2007 along with a friend from IIT, Binny Bansal (not related). Sachin was nowhere around at the Flipkart campus when the Walmart top team led by CEO Doug McMillon addressed employees in a town hall meeting Wednesday evening.

Another significant exit is that of Soft Bank, the largest investor in Flipkart. In a strange coincidence, the deal, valuing Flipkart at $20.8 billion, was announced to the world by Soft Bank Chief Executive Masayoshi Son in a webinar with investors hours before Walmart did so. He also confirmed that Soft Bank would get about $4 billion from its $2.5-billion investment in Flipkart last August.

Flipkart's valuation at $20.8 billion is a 75% increase over its previous valuation in the range of $11–12 billion last August. Out of the $16-billion investment, Walmart will put in $2 billion in new equity funding, while the rest will be utilized to acquire stakes of existing investors in the Bengaluru-based company.

Indian Business Case Studies. Sandeep Pachpande, Asha Pachpande, and J A Kulkarni, Oxford University Press.
© ASM Group of Institutes, Pune, India 2022. DOI: 10.1093/oso/9780192869371.003.0017

In a statement issued on Wednesday, Walmart said it would eventually look at the public listing of Flipkart as a majority-owned subsidiary though the company did not share a timeline for this. The Bentonville, Arkansas-headquartered company said the deal would be closed later in the current calendar year, subject to regulatory approvals. While the deal was being watched by world leaders, back home there were voices of protest. The RSS economic wing called it Walmart's backdoor entry into India, and traders' association CAIT argued the deal would 'vitiate Indian e-commerce'.

Retail majors, including Kishore Biyani of the Future group, too, watched the deal with interest and told Business Standard that strategic deals with online players would be the future of retail in India. The deal, advised by JP Morgan from the Walmart side and Goldman Sachs for Flipkart, would bring in the largest piece of FDI into India. This would give Walmart access to the fast-growing online retail space in the country. More than anything else, this would help Walmart fight its battle with rival Amazon, which lags behind Flipkart in terms of gross merchandise value (GMV). But the Indian authorities are already asking Walmart and Flipkart about the tax liabilities post the mega transaction. According to global research and analyst firm Forrester, India's e-commerce sector hit $19.2 billion in sales in 2017 and is expected to grow to $73 billion by 2022, at a compound annual growth rate of 30.62%.

Case Details

After the US and China, India is expected to be the next big market for online retail and is the last large, untapped market globally. 'India is one of the most attractive retail markets in the world, given its size and growth rate, and our investment is an opportunity to partner with the company that is leading transformation of e-Commerce in the market,' said Walmart's McMillon. 'Our investment will benefit India providing quality, affordable goods for customers, while creating new skilled jobs and fresh opportunities for small suppliers, farmers and women entrepreneurs,' he added.

Flipkart and Walmart also said they were in discussions with other investors to participate in the round without offering any details of who these additional investors could be. Insiders say, Alphabet, the parent company of Google, has shown interest to invest in the online retail firm and is in discussion with them. While further investments in Flipkart could bring down Walmart's overall stake in the company, it said that it would retain 'clear majority ownership'.

After the deal is closed, Binny Bansal, co-founder and Group CEO at Flipkart, will continue to hold the same position. 'Walmart is the ideal partner for the next phase of our journey, and we look forward to working together in the years ahead to bring our strengths and learning in retail and e-Commerce to the fore,' said Binny Bansal. 'This investment is of immense importance for India and will help fuel our ambition to deepen our connection with buyers and sellers and to create the next wave of retail in India.'

Flipkart's second largest shareholder, Tiger Global Management, will sell a large portion of its shares and retain a small holding in the company.

Walmart management reposed strong faith in the existing leadership at Flipkart and its subsidiaries including Myntra and PhonePe. Walmart said Tencent, Tiger Global, and Microsoft will continue to be its strategic and technology partners. Experts say Walmart still has an uphill task of competing with Amazon, which it has struggled to do on its own home turf in the US. Walmart can utilize its sourcing and retail prowess to aid Flipkart's efficiency, it still needed to come up with a product that can match Amazon's Prime loyalty programme.

While the deal gave Walmart access to India, which is the largest market outside of the US and China, its stock could continue to see pressure from investors post the deal. Unlike Amazon's investors who reward the company for diverting profits to win in new markets, Walmart's stock is significantly undervalued and they'd have to answer a lot more questions about their India investment considering Flipkart was still making losses. The company's stock was down 5.3% before the market opened in New York, and subsequently started recovering.

The Aftermath

The story of how two young men grew a small online bookstore called Flipkart into an e-commerce giant is one that Indian entrepreneurs will remember for years, even as the country's largest conglomerates possibly regret missing out on it.

Walmart's \$16-billion acquisition of a 77% stake in India's largest on-line marketplace is the world's biggest e-commerce deal. While this proves that Indian businesses are capable of offering stellar exits to investors, it also shows that the country has not been able to sustain local corporate champions.

The Flipkart-Walmart deal, entrepreneurs and investors hope, will be the trigger for domestic companies to look deeper into India's internet ecosystem, including financial technology, health technology, and artificial intelligence businesses. 'This is a big wake-up call for large Indian corporate houses. The fault is theirs for having stood on the sidelines,' said an investor in a consumer internet start-up, declining to be identified. 'Indian businessmen looked at the internet ecosystem with skepticism while foreigners saw value in it.'

Among Flipkart's top investors were Japanese internet conglomerate Soft Bank, South African media group Naspers, Chinese messaging app WeChat's parent company Tencent and US technology giant Microsoft. All of these have now exited Flipkart, fetching handsome returns from the Walmart deal.

Even if Flipkart may have become too big for Indian companies to back, investors say there were several other opportunities in recent years for local corporate giants to participate in the country's commerce boom.

Moreover, backing internet companies across sectors would have been a good investment thesis, not just in terms of financial returns but also as a means to adapt and learn from an emerging technology to stay relevant, say investors and entrepreneurs.

'Some of the top 10 Fortune 500 companies in the US are tech companies. In the next 10 years from India, how will that happen? Other industries are equally important but the market cap will come from tech companies,' said K Ganesh, founder of start-up incubator GrowthStory. 'Those who invested in Flipkart are those who took the bold bets instead of criticising valuations and unit economics. Unless one takes bold bets how will you play the market later?'

Increase in Capital Flow

The Flipkart-Walmart deal is likely to increase the flow of capital into the domestic ecosystem, as limited partners globally reopen their purses with renewed confidence in one of the fastest-growing developing markets. Limited partners are investors in venture capital and other funds. This expected surge in capital, however, would play a limited role in stoking interest among individuals to start businesses, unlike in 2014–2015 when increased flow brought with it a surge in start-up formation, said experts.

About 13,685 start-ups were formed in India in 2015, of which about 20% were e-commerce companies, as India's internet ecosystem undertook a massive clean-up in terms of both quality of businesses and quantity of capital invested, that number nosedived to 2,671.

Exit Options

Flipkart's sale is also expected to give start-up founders the confidence to go against the tide, with the deal establishing India as a potentially hot market for more such investment exits.

'The valuation outcome that Flipkart has garnered (of nearly $21 billion) has blown past even that of an IPO. This is a signal for entrepreneurs to not rush into an IPO because there are better exits if one disrupts the market enough, does not cede ground and attempts to gain market share whatever be the cost.' 'Value does not lie only in having a profitable IPO-led business. Flipkart has shown that.'

The deal marks the largest exit for investors in India's technology landscape. Investors cashing out of Flipkart are expected to collectively fetch about $14 billion when the deal completes, answering long-held doubts on if investments in Indian start-ups would yield results.

Investors believe that the deal marks the first step towards the creation of a more mature market where one can see more exits spread across a larger number of companies and consistently so, over the next few years. 'If you look at a market like Israel, over the past five years, they have consistently had exits in technology companies cumulatively amounting to over $40 billion across 300 VC- and PE-backed firms.'

Of Angels and Mafias

The $500-million bounty that Flipkart employees are in for from the Walmart deal presents a potential bounty for the larger ecosystem as well. About 100 current and former Flipkart employees with ESOPs are now estimated to be worth more than $1 million. A good part of that money could flow back into the start-up ecosystem as some of these now wealthy individuals may turn investors and entrepreneurs themselves.

Industry executives see the Flipkart-Walmart deal as a turning point for India's angel investing ecosystem, even if just $100 million from liquidated ESOPs is invested back into start-ups. 'The Flipkart Angel Group is one of the more powerful emerging angel investor groups in the ecosystem.'

The emergence of such a large capital pool is particularly timely given the steady dip in angel and seed investments that the ecosystem has witnessed over the last three years. Data from Venture Intelligence show a slow recovery in the first four months of 2018 with $62 million in angel investments.

Flipkart's acquisition is likely to hasten that pace and bring the zing back in angel investing, say experts. Former Flipkart employees such as Sujeet Kumar of logistics firm Udaan and Curefit founder Mukesh Bansal are expected to be some of the biggest beneficiaries of cashing out from Flipkart. That's apart from Sachin Bansal, who is exiting the company, founded with a $1 billion harvest from selling his shares to Walmart. Mukesh Bansal's Curefit is one of the foremost examples of the so-called Flipkart Mafia, with the fitness chain counting Myntra CEO Ananth Narayanan, Flipkart co-founder Binny Bansal, and CEO Kalyan Krishnamurthy as angel investors.

Mukesh Bansal was a founding member of online fashion retailer Myntra, which Flipkart bought in 2014. With over 200 start-ups founded by former Flipkart employees and over $200 million invested in these start-ups, this 'Flipkart Mafia' is set to further grow, leaving behind it a far richer ecosystem of start-ups, investors, and serial entrepreneurs.

Walmart's Low Pricing Model Worries Sellers

Sellers on Flipkart are already apprehensive that Walmart will bring its global everyday low pricing business model on general merchandise to the marketplace, indulging in deep discounting.

However, the deal could also give Flipkart an improved supply chain and make it more process-oriented, which will help it to compete with Amazon, some sellers said. The real fight will be in food retailing, where 100% foreign direct investment is allowed and Amazon has government approval to start this business. Although India doesn't allow online marketplaces such as Flipkart and Amazon to influence the prices of products sold on their platforms, sellers have objected to units of these e-commerce companies selling their private labels at discounts.

The 'Every Day Low Costs, Every Day Low Prices' offer, which has made Walmart the world's top retailer, could add to the competitive pressure on smaller online sellers and drive them out of business. They fear getting squeezed between the two giants—the Walmart-Flipkart combine and Amazon—even though consumers will benefit.

'Walmart has global purchase power that gives it a big advantage in terms of costs,' said Vishwas Shringi, cofounder at Voylla Retail, a large fashion and lifestyle products seller on online marketplaces including Flipkart.

'They can come and disrupt the entire market with their "everyday low pricing offer." This will definitely put pressure on sellers as they would now compete with Walmart predatory pricing, which is impossible to beat.' An electronics seller fears the Walmart-Flipkart deal will once again bring back insanity into discounting, at least in the short run.

'Deep discounts had become limited to only major sales. But the deal may increase discounting and would also sway Amazon into it. This may happen for at least the first few months since Walmart would want to show its supremacy,' said the seller, requesting anonymity.

Walmart May Step Up India Sourcing for Global Market

Walmart will likely step-up sourcing from India for its global operations as the Flipkart acquisition gives it access to the huge supplier base of the e-commerce company. The US-based retailer currently sources goods worth over a 'couple of billion' dollars, such as apparel, generic medicines, and handicrafts, from Indian suppliers such as Welspun and Dr Reddy's for its stores in the US, UK, Canada, and South America.

Walmart's sourcing from India is still small compared with that from China, which ships some $50 billion worth of goods to the company's stores, but the combination of its best price cash and carry business and Flipkart is now expected to help boost India's contribution. The bigger base of suppliers from Flipkart will offer it more opportunities to source for its retail outlets abroad, while also allowing the suppliers a wider exposure to overseas markets. While Flipkart had an association with eBay to take sellers global as eBay cashed out and decided to relaunch its website.

Walmart said it would support small businesses and 'Make in India' through direct procurement as well as provide increased opportunities for exports through global sourcing and e-commerce. Analysts said the India market opportunity for Walmart will in fact be meatier than that from building a larger supply chain to source goods for global markets. 'Nothing was stopping them from sourcing (from India) anyways. Walmart might increase it a little bit more.

They are going to bring a lot of products from outside to Indian customers, which they were not able to sell earlier. They will now channel that in India through Flipkart.' Walmart has over 20 best price cash and carries outlets in India. In fiscal 2017, the India unit posted revenue of Rs 3,641crore, of which two-thirds came from sales of food and groceries.

Walmart's sourcing and negotiating power for best price is what Flipkart is looking for, said Meena, adding that the Indian retailer could 'get an edge on food and private' labels with the deal. 'Between cash and carry business and Flipkart, Walmart will focus more on India. They have the backend systems and expertise in large-scale sourcing. They will focus on expanding the 100 million (Flipkart) customers.' Walmart is also looking to consolidate its India operations in Bengaluru, where Flipkart is based.

Walmart Opens a New Front in Global Battle with Amazon

Walmart's acquisition of a controlling stake in Flipkart has raised several questions on the future of India's largest online retailer.

For the fiscal year 2016–2017, Flipkart reported a 29% increase in revenue to Rs 19,854 crore, but the report had two red flags. The first was that revenue growth had slowed from 50% in the prior year, and the second was that Flipkart's loss had increased 68% to Rs 8,771 crore. In spite of that, Tiger Global, Flipkart's largest investor until recently, priced the company at nearly $18 billion when it invested $424 million in it in January, an astounding rise in value for a company started in 2007 with Rs 6 lakh in capital. Walmart is paying $16 billion for 77% of Flipkart, valuing the company at nearly $21 billion.

It is no secret that Walmart has been eyeing the Indian market for a while, recognizing the potential for growth in retailing here. But attempts to enter this market for much of the last few decades have not been successful. At the start of 2018, Walmart owned 21 stores in India, a small profile for a market the size of India. The most direct explanation for Walmart's acquisition of Flipkart is that it gives the company a significant foothold in India's online retail market, and perhaps benefit Walmart's brick-and-mortar retail investments in the country.

Given that Flipkart is losing substantial amounts already, the potential for increased income is minimal, at least in the near term. You would need a big boost from the combination to justify the premium. It is, therefore, no surprise that many observers, looking at the deal standing alone, and given that Walmart is more likely to be investing money into the deal rather than taking money out, have concluded that Walmart is paying too much for too little.

A simpler explanation for the Walmart gambit and it has its roots in a global battle that Walmart is involved in with Amazon. Amazon is the most fearsome competitor on the face of the earth, and has been successful at laying to waste entire businesses. In fact, when Amazon announces plans to enter a new business, the market routinely knocks down the values of competitors in that business by 10% or more. In the brick-and-mortar retail business in the US, Amazon's conquest is almost complete, with Walmart remaining its only major rival.

In fact, Walmart is one of the few companies that has been able to go head-to-head against Amazon in online retailing in the US, with its acquisition of Wayfair, an online retailer. Walmart has been watching Amazon's aggressive investment in India with trepidation, concerned that Amazon will make its control of Indian online retailing complete by either driving

Flipkart out of business or acquiring it, putting at risk Walmart's long-term plan of opening brick-and-mortar retail stores in the country.

Put differently, Walmart's acquisition of Flipkart fundamentally seems to be a defensive manoeuvre, where Walmart is engaging Amazon in India by supplying badly needed capital to Flipkart to continue in business, with the promise of more if needed. Walmart's war with Amazon is fought on many fronts and in many geographies, and ceding a market as big as India to Amazon would set Walmart back in that global battle. Viewed in that perspective, where you have hundreds of billions of dollars in play, a multibillion premium paid on an acquisition is penny change. This battle among multinational behemoths also explains why Google is also a player in this acquisition, since it, too, fears Amazon's entry into its business space.

This acquisition will open the floodgates to even more intense competition in the online retail space in India, and both Walmart and Amazon will lose more money in the near term as a consequence. The beneficiaries, though, will be Indian consumers who will wake up to better deals, lower shipping costs, and expedited service, as the two giants open their pockets. Let the good times roll!

What Walmart Will Do Next after Buying in India, Selling in UK

Walmart has agreed to cede control of its British business to a competitor and spend $16 billion to acquire Flipkart. The sun never sets on Walmart Inc.'s empire, thanks to its network of stores across five continents. But in the span of 10 days, Chief Executive Doug McMillon has begun dramatically redrawing the retailer's map, and there's likely more to come as it places bets to remain on top.

In less than two weeks, Walmart has agreed to cede control of its British business to a competitor and spend $16 billion to acquire India's e-commerce leader in its biggest-ever deal, fending off Amazon.com Inc. The wheeling and dealing show how McMillon is focusing on high-potential markets like China and India, finding partners to help it battle online and cutting loose middling businesses. He's got more work to do, though, and subpar markets like Brazil and Japan might be next on his list.

Walmart's far-flung international units don't get much attention, but they're important as a source of cash, management talent, and ideas that percolate into its core US operations. Sales growth outside the US once topped more than 10% annually, adjusted for currency moves, but it's less than half that now as sluggish economies, store closures, and fierce competition have taken their toll.

Those pressures—combined with a US e-commerce business that continues to spill red ink and higher labour expenses from this year's wage hike—have forced McMillon into hard choices. Some, like selling the British Asda stores, were welcomed by Wall Street, but Wednesday's deal got a rude welcome from investors, who raised concerns about Flipkart's steep losses and asked whether Walmart's cash would be better spent elsewhere. S&P Global Ratings said the heavy spending to compete with Amazon could threaten Walmart's pristine credit rating. McMillon defended the Flipkart deal to analysts, saying it was a unique opportunity. He's certainly mindful of past missteps abroad, such as his 2011 decision to buy an unprofitable, second-tier online marketplace in China that's forced the company to play catch-up to Alibaba—the Amazon of China—ever since.

Walmart's international reach sprawls across 6,360 stores in about two dozen countries from Argentina to Zambia. Many were acquired during a buying spree from 1999 to 2009, but that era of aggressive flag-planting is long over. Today the international business accounts for less than one-quarter of Walmart's total revenue, down from nearly 30% five years ago. That share will decline further after Walmart's decision to merge its Asda business in the UK with Sainsbury Plc, retreating from a market that was once its shining star abroad. Other moves are expected to follow, as the Asda sale 'was the first volley' in a broader reshuffle of Walmart's global holdings, said Mark Stoeckle, portfolio manager of the Adams Diversified Equity Fund, which owns Walmart shares.

Stoeckle and other investors were encouraged when Walmart's finance chief, Brett Biggs, said in October that he's 'open to taking action' to simplify operations. Getting leaner should help Walmart devote more focus and firepower to its escalating battle with Amazon, which is trying to crack categories like food and apparel, long Walmart strongholds. Acquiring e-commerce start-up Jet.com two years ago has helped, but the Flipkart deal suggests that future moves will likely come outside the US.

Case Questions

1. Do you think that Walmart is hell-bent on entering the Indian retail market in spite of restrictions imposed by Government of India on foreign companies investing in multi-brand retail market (single brand has no such restrictions)? And this is the main reason of 77% takeover bid of Flipkart?

2. Walmart has been in India since nearly a decade in B2-B Market and in establishing its supply chain technology projects at the back office of many Indian e-commerce companies. Now once the merger/take over is cleared by the competition committee of India Walmart could use the existing outlets of Flipkart to exploit its own multi-brand products in India through its Flipkart outlets since strategically they have decided to keep Flipkarts business and networks independent even after it gets all clearances. Of what specific interest is this merger to Indian retail market?

3. Walmart has many class action suits pending against it challenging its work practices and exploitation of its workforce of issues related to inhuman work environment and discrimination against communities. How do you rate this possibility in India with its glaring unemployment levels and social issues?

18

Hyundai and Kia—The Journey of the Twins

A Case Study in Operations Management and International Marketing

Learning Objectives

To understand the capital structure pattern of Hyundai Motor Company with reference to the generation platform. To study the Hyundai-Kia Motor Company Corporate operations—Corporate structure, shareholder strategies, R&D strategies, localization strategies, production capabilities, and performance overview. To understand the forecasted steady growth of the global auto market with reference to the generation platform. To understand the effort to increase production capacity of Kia and Hyundai with reference to the generation platform. To study the success of the company's growth based on reasonably priced vehicles, improved product quality year-over-year, constant introduction of new vehicles to the market, targeted product portfolios for the different global customer groups. To understand in this case: brand crisis, brand reputation, market share, perception, competitiveness, competitive advantage, growth strategy.

Synopsis

Hyundai Motor Company started in 1967 and in 1975, in partnership with Ford Motor Company, produced the Hyundai Cortina. With

Indian Business Case Studies. Sandeep Pachpande, Asha Pachpande, and J A Kulkarni, Oxford University Press. © ASM Group of Institutes, Pune, India 2022. DOI: 10.1093/oso/9780192869371.003.0018

overseas talent, the first models were designed and became successful in some occidental countries. Sales were developing and Hyundai was becoming a great option for a market that loved to save. Now it is a top competitor in the automobile manufacturing, positioned in quality and gas-saving.

Kia, headquartered in Seoul, is South Korea's second-largest automobile manufacturer, following the Hyundai Motor Company, with sales of over 2.7 million vehicles in 2012 and almost 2.75 million vehicles in 2013. Kia's first manufacturing plant in Mexico, located in Pesqueria, Nuevo Leon (near Monterrey), will boast an annual production capacity of 300,000 units. The popular Forte sedan will be the first model to be produced at the Kia Motors Mexico plant and when the plant enters operation, Kia's global manufacturing capacity will be boosted to 3.37 million vehicles.

Brief History about Hyundai

The Hyundai Motor Company was set up in 1967 as a subsidiary of the Hyundai Engineering and Construction Company. The company started off by assembling cars and trucks for the Ford Company in their car factory. In 1975 they produced their first car called the Hyundai Cortina which was produced in partnership with the Ford Motor Company. Within the next two years they had become the 13th largest automaker in the world with 2% share in the world retail market.

In 1975, the company decided to build its own car which it would sell under the brand name 'Hyundai'. They hired five of the best car engineers from Britain who designed their first car, 'Hyundai Pony'. The car soon became the number one selling car in South Korea because of its small size and economical pricing. Next the Hyundai Pony entered the Canadian market and within nine months became the top-selling car there. By 1985, their production had exceeded more than 1 million cars.

In 1986, they entered the US market with their new 'Hyundai Excel' car. This car also proved to be a best seller because of its quality and low pricing. In 1986 more than 160,000 units were sold and the next year it crossed 260,000. Now Hyundai had established itself as one of the top competitors in the world automobile industry. Their next release was the midsize Sonata in the year 1988. This model did not click in the US market but by then Hyundai was already producing 4,000,000 units per year.

Hyundai restructured themselves by investing heavily in the quality, design, research, and manufacturing of its vehicles. As a result they came up with the first proprietary gasoline engine with its own transmission including the four-cylinder Alpha. They started giving a 10-year or 10,000-mile warranty for all their cars sold in the US. This improved their image and prompted more and more customers to choose a Hyundai car over other brands.

It continued its success with the release of best-selling cars like the Hyundai Elantra, Hyundai Tucson, Hyundai Santa Fe, and Hyundai Genesis. Hyundai has been in receipt of many awards over the years for its cars' durability and fuel efficiency.

By 1995, Hyundai had set up sales in countries like Australia, New Zealand, Egypt, and Japan where it released country-specific models according to customer requirements. In 1998, Hyundai purchased a 51% stake in Kia Motors which was then the second-largest automobile manufacturer in South Korea. By the year 2000, it had manufacturing plants in India, China, Pakistan, Turkey, and Czech Republic. In 2004, the company had $56 billion in revenue with sales of more than 2,500,000 units. By the year 2011, Hyundai sold more than 4.04 million cars making it the fourth largest car maker in the world behind GM, Volkswagen, and Toyota.

In 2012, Hyundai sold 4.5 million vehicles worldwide and together with their subsidiary Kia total sales exceeded 7 million units. As of 2013, Hyundai produces more than 3,000,000 units every year in its plants spread across the world. It has more than $ 82 billion in revenue and nearly 75,000 employees. From taking a cautious start in the automobile industry, Hyundai has today become one of the most trusted four-wheeler brands in the world. Hyundai's success has been a result of its continuous focus on expansion and customer satisfaction.

Making History in Mexico

Hyundai Motor México entered the Mexican market in 2014 with the Hyundai Grand i10, the Hyundai Elantra, and the Hyundai ix35. Soon afterwards, the Hyundai Sonata joined the line-up. Prior to the introduction of the Hyundai brand for non-commercial vehicles, Hyundai passenger vehicles, light-duty cargo vans, and passenger vans were distributed by Chrysler de México, branded as Dodge.

Mexico is rapidly becoming the go-to place for North American auto production, and companies including Toyota, General Motors, and Audi are all building new plants, expanding, or shifting some production there. Now, Hyundai is investigating joining them in the future.

'I'm sure that over the years we'll see production of Hyundai products in Mexico,' Pedro Albarran, managing director for the automaker in Mexico, said to Bloomberg. Albarran indicates that a likely location for such a factory might be the state of Nuevo León, where Kia also has a forthcoming $1 billion plant. The site would be an ideal location near suppliers.

It's probably going to be a while before any of Hyundai's models start coming out of Mexico. According to Bloomberg, the automaker wants to wait to make a final decision until sales there reach around 50,000 annual units, and that benchmark isn't expected until 2018.

While Kia's plant is slated to have a capacity of around 300,000 vehicles a year when it opens in 2016, Albarran thinks Hyundai might start smaller at just over 100,000 annual examples. Some of those would likely include subcompact models for the Mexican market. The Korean automaker was rumoured to be looking into a factory south of the border as far back as 2013.

Kia Motors Corp does not aim to share its planned Mexico plant with its sister South Korean carmaker Hyundai Motor Co, its Mexico chief said.

Hyundai Motor has been selling cars in Mexico for a little over a year and has already made significant inroads in Latin America's second-largest economy. May sales figures show that the South Korean automaker's efforts to sell Sonata sedans and ix35 crossovers to middle-class residents in Mexico's larger cities are rapidly paying off.

Hyundai recently began focusing on Latin America in an effort to snatch regional market share from smaller players, such as Suzuki and Mazda. In recent years, the company has focused on the Americas and Asia while relying less on growth in Europe, where Hyundai had trouble competing against entrenched domestic brands at a time of regional economic strife. Recent economic troubles in Brazil, Argentina, and Venezuela have made Mexico the most ideal Latin American location to stimulate local sales.

Data from the Mexican Automotive Industry Association (AMIA) released Tuesday shows Hyundai is on pace to overtake Renault this year as Mexico's ninth-largest seller of new cars. Hyundai expects to nearly double Mexican sales in 2015 to 22,000 units.

Hyundai's annual global revenue has grown 33% since 2010, from $59.9 billion to $79.8 billion last year.

Hyundai delivered 2,049 new vehicles to Mexican buyers last month and 8,532 for the year, according to AIMA's data, putting it right behind Renault's 8,660 units. While these numbers are much smaller than the biggest players in Mexico—Nissan has sold more than 132,000 vehicles in the first five months of the year—they show the strength of Hyundai's sales, which amounted to only 705 units in May 2014, the month it set up its local Mexico City headquarters.

Hyundai used to sell sedans in Mexico under a deal with Chrysler Group, which sold them under the more recognizable Dodge brand name. But that deal ended in 2013, when Hyundai decided it had enough brand recognition to go at it alone in Latin America.

Like its rivals, Hyundai sees Mexico as a lucrative and low-cost manufacturing platform for building and sending cars abroad through the country's web of free-trade agreements.

'Hyundai wants to turn Mexico into a very important base for its global production,' Pedro Albarran, Hyundai's head of Mexico sales, told Bloomberg in April. The company eventually will build a Mexican factory once sales hit 50,000 a year, which is expected in 2018, according to Automotive News. But Albarran has said the company currently has no specific plans.

Hyundai is focusing on a Mexican retail footprint to nurture a domestic appetite for South Korean imported cars in a market expected to grow 3% to 1.16 million new-vehicle purchases this year, according to IHS Automotive.

Monterrey as the Promised Land

The plant, being built in northern Mexico for over $1 billion, is due to begin operations in 2016 and will service the United States, Mexican, and South American markets, producing 300,000 cars per year, said

Kia Mexico Chief Executive Horacio Chavez. Kia, which is due to begin selling cars in Mexico in July, has been seen by analysts as a potential partner for Hyundai, whose executives have said they are 'actively' seeking greater US capacity. But Kia does not plan to share the plant with Hyundai, said Chavez, who expects to sell 9,000 cars in Mexico in 2015.

'Each company takes a different route, each one has its own strategy,' Chavez said. Kia and Hyundai Motor Company are both owned by Hyundai Motor Group in South Korea.

Around 60% of Kia's planned production in Mexico will be exported to the United States, around 20% to South America and the remainder to Mexico, he said. Hyundai's Mexico head said last month the company was not planning on building a factory in the country. Sonata, Elantra, and Santa Fe are their biggest products yet.

Nevertheless, recalls and warranties have been a constant issue in their way to success.

Bumps on the Road

Hyundai notched big gains in its sales, market share, and image when its swoopy 2011 Sonata hit the market. But barely three years later, the midsized Sonata left Hyundai with a black eye.

Problems reported by owners of the 2011 Sonata were the main reason that the Hyundai brand ranked fifth from the bottom in the latest dependability rankings from J.D. Power and Associates. Also, in 2015 Hyundai is recalling nearly 130,000 Sonatas over an issue with the seatbelt buckle. According to a recall bulletin from the National Highway Traffic Safety Administration (NHTSA), 128,804 Sonatas built for the 2015 model year are being called back for front passenger seatbelts that may not work.

Hyundai is recalling almost 205,000 of its Elantra cars because the power steering could suddenly stop working, making the vehicle harder to turn, according to a report from the automaker posted on Saturday on the NHTSA's website.

The action covers the 2008–2010 Elantra and the 2009–2010 Elantra Touring. Hyundai said the driver would still be able to steer the car if the power steering was lost but that it would require 'greater driver effort,' particularly at low speeds. The automaker did not mention any accidents or injuries related to the issue.

Hyundai owners reported an average of 169 problems per 100 vehicles in J.D. Power's 2014 Vehicle Dependability Study, which measures the performance of vehicles after three years of ownership. It was Hyundai's second year of increasing problems after steady improvement from 2009 to 2012.

Also contributing to the low scores was Hyundai's Elantra compact car, J.D. Power said. The current generation of both cars launched as 2011 models from Hyundai's plant in Alabama, which has been running around the clock on three shifts since the fall of 2012.

Not Holding Up

The Hyundai brand finished 27th, or 5th from the bottom, in this year's J.D. Power Vehicle Dependability Study rankings. The study measures the average number of problems per 100 vehicles reported by owners who have owned their cars for three years.

Chung Eui-sun, vice chairman of Hyundai Motor Co., visited the plant and Ed Kim, an analyst with consultancy Auto Pacific, says the dependability shortcomings are unlikely to hurt Hyundai's brand in the near term. Kim says most consumers pay closer attention to J.D. Power's initial-quality rankings. However, customers are getting very upset and throwing their frustration at their social media profiles. Still, he says, the poor dependability scores are a red flag for a brand that has put years of work into improving its quality reputation.

'We've finally reached the point where people have far fewer prejudices against Hyundai's quality,' Kim said. He added: 'The poor VDS performance is a warning sign to Hyundai because it takes a lot of time and money to build and rebuild a reputation for quality, which they've successfully done for a long time since introducing their 100,000-mile warranty. But it can be destroyed in a flash.'

In a statement, a Hyundai Motor Co. representative said the company is 'very disappointed' by the results, adding that it 'is in the process of examining every component of the score to determine root-cause

Table 18.1 Vehicle dependability study rankings

Study year/ Model year	Problems per 100 Vehicles	Industry Rank	Rank among Non-Luxury Brands
2009/2006	161*	14	4
2010/2007	148*	11	4
2011/2008	132*	10	2
2012/2009	125*	10	4
2013/2010	141	22	13
2014/2011	169	27	13

*Better than industry average

solutions and improve our products and processes'. A Hyundai quality executive was unavailable to comment last week.

It's not uncommon for vehicles to have problems in their launch year, but the Sonata launch had more problems than usual for Hyundai and for the industry in general, said Dave Sargent, J.D. Power's vice president of automotive, who leads the annual study. The Sonata was a game-changing vehicle for the Hyundai brand when it arrived as a 2011 model, with a distinctive design that shook up the otherwise staid mid-sized sedan segment. It soon became Hyundai's top-selling car.

Such success can be a double-edged sword, especially if durability problems persist, says Karl Brauer, senior analyst at Kelley Blue Book. 'That car was at the heart of a lot of the momentum that they were seeing at the same time that their image, sales and everything was getting better', Brauer said. 'You don't want any of your cars to have a bad reputation, but it would be far better if it was something more obscure from their model line.'

Sargent declined to identify the main issues that drove the Sonata complaints. But for the industry in general, the J.D. Power study found a rise in engine and transmission problems, especially for four-cylinder engines. 'While striving to reduce fuel consumption, automakers must be careful not to compromise quality', Sargent said in a statement when the study was released. 'Increases in such problems as engine hesitation, rough transmission shifts and lack of power indicate that this is a continuing challenge.'

The 2011 Sonata ushered in advanced power train technologies that were rare in the segment at the time, such as all-aluminium engines, gasoline direct injection, six-speed transmissions, and continuously variable valve timing. It was also the first mid-sized sedan to use a turbocharged four-cylinder in place of a V-6 for high-end models.

In its statement, Hyundai said it expects its dependability ratings to improve in next year's J.D. Power study.

Auto Pacific's Kim noted that Hyundai has prioritized improving vehicle quality over growing sales volume for the past few years. 'Knowing them,' he said, 'I'm sure they're not sitting still.'

Toyota Investing $1 Billion in Mexico Plant

Toyota announced today that it will build a new plant in Mexico and expand its joint venture, Guangzhou Toyota Motor Co., Ltd. (GTMC), in China. These investments are grounded on its plans to construct production lines that are more competitive, with greatly reduced initial investment, improved efficiency, flexibility, environmental performance, and safety. These 'simple and slim' production lines can be easily lengthened or shortened depending on demand. Over-head conveyance devices are eliminated, compact equipment is installed on top of the plant floors, and paint-booths are smaller.

The new plant in Mexico and the expansion in China will be designed to accelerate innovation by implementing these new technologies into real production lines.

With today's announcement, Akio Toyoda, president of Toyota Motor Corporation, said: 'This investment represents our long-held principles of continuous improvement and challenging ourselves to always do better. An increase in production does not mean an undisciplined pursuit of more. Toyota's expansion must be driven by providing ever-better-cars and our talented people. These investments will be an important test of Toyota's resolve and a measure of tangible improvement.'

Toyota had previously suspended construction of new plants in order to improve capacity utilization of existing plants and plan for reduced model change-over and new plant construction investment. Currently, total capacity utilization is more than 90% and the initial portion of new simple and slim plant costs, including structure and equipment, is expected to be approximately 40% lower when compared to 2008. Toyota is taking these steps considering the achievements and forecasted steady growth of the global auto market.

Outcome

The result evident from the case above is that for the brands to be globally known and to be preferred brand worldwide we need to focus upon TQM (Total Quality Management). For brands success in the global market we need to do Swotify the market in a better way so as to maintain the sustainability with the existing competitors. All it depends upon the strategies we decide to target the different markets on the international platform. To penetrate globally we need to analyse the brand's competitive strengths so as to fight with the competitors and maintain the goodwill of being a successful brand for a longer period of time.

Conclusions

Hyundai and Kia have so far made good success under the relatively protected condition of domestic market and with the export of their low-priced cars to overseas market. Under the rapidly changing environment this auto group's survival to further enhance its own technological capability of R&D and manufacturing operations as well as improve the quality and reliability of its products, which is a necessary condition for upgrading the competitiveness of its car brands. In addition, as it has tried since the merger, the Hyundai-Kia group needs to nurture its auto parts suppliers 'technological and financial capability', which has been much poorer than those in advanced countries. Hyundai and Kia have maintained the duplicate business positioning of their car models. Both companies have expressed a strong interest in keeping intact the existing business composition, covering the full range of car models, in contrast with the top management's long-term intention to separate business segments between the two automakers, thus, in case of trying to introduce a new group-wide business frame having each of the two automakers focus on different segments of auto sales and manufacturing.

Case Questions

1. What do you think are the real issues involved for the difference of views in merger of Hyundai, Kia as explained in the case?

2. Do you think a merger between Kia and Hyundai would be in the interest of both and why?

3. How do you think the issues about warranties and recalls will affect Hyundai business expansion in the main countries it is trying to reach?

4. Which manufacturing problems do you think Hyundai should resolve before increasing their production?

19

What Happened to Old McDonald's?

A Case Study in Brand Management and Strategy Management

Learning Objectives

To understand the capital structure pattern of McDonald's restaurants; American capitalism's greatest success stories, reputable brand image, and a memorable history. To understand the main objectives of McDonald's for adapting to the changing demand of its customers and the customers' perception of McDonald's food quality. To understand the maintenance of the traditional efficiency of fast-food restaurants and provide comfortable environment to customers and changing market demand and standards. To study the McDonald's branding strategy, marketing strategy, market analysis and market share model. To understand the McDonald's brand crisis, reputation, PR and crisis management, market segmentation, product development, market development, and the main reason/ reasons for a big corporation to fall.

Synopsis

McDonald's, the seemingly invincible fast-food giant and stalwart of American business, has been an ironclad money-making machine for decades now. Sure, they've had their issues with bad press concerning the negative health effects of their food, but otherwise the company is as sure to post profits quarter after quarter as anyone. At least that's been true

Indian Business Case Studies. Sandeep Pachpande, Asha Pachpande, and J A Kulkarni, Oxford University Press.
© ASM Group of Institutes, Pune, India 2022. DOI: 10.1093/oso/9780192869371.003.0019

until recently, as it appears that McDonald's has hit a bit of a snag. Starting out with just one burger stall in 1948, the fast-food chain's emphasis on quick service and a standardized menu has helped it to grow to more than 35,000 outlets across the world. It has been profitable: after a wobbly period in the early 2000s, the firm's share price went from $12 in 2003 to more than $100 at the end of 2011. But now McDonald's has lost its sizzle. Global sales have been declining at least since last July. When the company announces its annual results on 23 January, analysts think it will reveal its first full-year fall in like-for-like revenues since 2002.

What's Gone Wrong?

Some of McDonald's problems stem from operational mishaps across the world. In particular, its business in Asia—where it makes nearly a quarter of its global revenues—has been hit by several health scares. Sales in China fell sharply after one of its suppliers was discovered last July to be using expired and contaminated chicken and beef. More recently, several Japanese customers have reported finding bits of plastic and even a tooth in their food. Geopolitics has not helped. Last year some Russian outlets were temporarily closed by food inspectors, seemingly, in retaliation for American and European sanctions against Russia over its military intervention in Ukraine.

Some politicians in Russia have even called for the chain to be thrown out of the country completely. But McDonald's also has problems at home. It faces competition from other fast-food chains such as Burger King, which has been gaining market share with a simpler and cheaper version of the McDonald's menu. And it is being squeezed by more up market 'fast-casual' restaurants such as Shake Shack and Chipotle Mexican Grill, which are rapidly growing. They have been luring customers—particularly younger ones—away from McDonald's chicken nuggets and chips by offering slightly better quality food, a high level of customization (such as the option to choose the ingredients in a burrito or burger) and some table service. McDonald's seems to have two options: to emulate the likes of Burger King and go back to basics, or to spruce itself up to compete with the likes of Shake Shack. The chain seems to be trying to do both. It now has two new formats, one offering a simpler menu, and another called 'Create your taste', letting customers customize their burgers. Similarly, it has opened 'Mc Cafés' in several countries. In France, one of the few parts of the world where McDonald's sales are still rising, these offer macaroons, tea, and coffee in China cups and saucers, as well as some limited waitress service. It hasn't always gone smoothly: some of the restaurants in Paris were forced to put signs on the bins saying 'please do not throw away the crockery'. As McDonald's tries to reinvent itself, it may find that disposing of its traditional image will prove much harder.

In a brand-new McDonald's outlet near its headquarters in Oak Brook, Illinois, customers do not have to queue at the counter. They can go to a touch screen and build their own burger by choosing a bun, toppings, and sauces from a list of more than 20 'premium' ingredients, including grilled mushrooms, guacamole, and caramelized onions. Then they sit down, waiting an average of seven minutes until a server brings their burgers to their table. The company is planning to roll out its 'Create Your Taste' burgers in up to 2,000 restaurants—it is not saying where—by late 2015, and possibly in more places if they do well.

McDonald's is also trying to engage with customers on social media and is working on a smartphone app, as well as testing mobile-payment systems such as Apple Pay, Soft card, and Google Wallet. All this is part of the 'Experience of the Future', a plan to revive the flagging popularity of McDonald's, especially among younger consumers. 'We are taking decisive action to change fundamentally the way we approach our business,' says Heidi Barker, a spokeswoman.

After a successful run which lifted the firm's share price from $12 in 2003 to more than $100 at the end of 2011, McDonald's had a tricky 2013 and a much harder time last year. When it announces its annual results on 23 January, some analysts fear it will reveal a drop in global 'like-for-like' sales (i.e., after stripping out the effect of opening new outlets) for the whole of 2014—the first such fall since 2002.

In the past year, Don Thompson, the firm's relatively new boss, has had to fight fires around the world, some of them beyond his control. Sales in China fell sharply after a local meat supplier was found guilty of using expired, contaminated chicken and beef. The biggest problem has been in America—by far McDonald's largest market, where it has 14,200 of its 35,000 mostly franchised restaurants. In November its American like-for-like sales were down 4.6% a year earlier.

It had weathered the 2008–2009 recession and its aftermath by attracting cash-strapped consumers looking for a cheap bite. But more recently, it has been squeezed by competition from Burger King, revitalized under the management of a private-equity firm, from other fast-food joints such as Subway and Starbucks, and from the growing popularity of slightly more up market 'fast casual' outlets. In response, McDonald's has expanded its menu with all manner of wraps, salads, and so on. Its American menu now has almost 200 items. This strains kitchen staff and annoys franchisees, who often have to buy new equipment. It may also deter customers. 'McDonald's stands for value, consistency and convenience,' says Darren Tristano at Technomic, a restaurant-industry consultant, and it needs to stay true to this. Most diners want a Big Mac or a Quarter Pounder at a good price, served quickly. And, as company executives now acknowledge, its strategy of reeling in diners with a 'Dollar Menu' then trying to tempt them with pricier dishes is not working.

McDonald's says it has got the message and is experimenting in some parts of America with a simpler menu: one type of Quarter Pounder with cheese rather than four; one Snack Wrap rather than three; and so on. However, this seems to run contrary to the build-your-burger strategy it is trying elsewhere, which expands the number of choices. That in turn is McDonald's response to the popularity of 'better burger' chains, such as Shake Shack, which has just filed for stock market floatation. Some analysts think that McDonald's should stop trying to replicate all its rivals' offerings and go back to basics, offering a limited range of dishes at low prices, served freshly and quickly.

Sara, Senator of Sanford, C. Bernstein, a research outfit, notes that Burger King, having struggled against its big rival for years, has begun to do better with a simpler and cheaper version of the McDonald's menu. For the third quarter of 2014 Burger King reported a like-for-like sales increase of 3.6% in America and Canada compared with a decrease of 3.3% of comparable sales at McDonald's. That said, sales at an average McDonald's in America are still roughly double those of an average Burger King. So the case for going back to basics remains unproven.

So far, McDonald's looks as if it is undergoing a milder version of its last crisis, in 2002–2003. Then, an over-rapid expansion had damaged its reputation for good service, its menu had become bloated and customers were drifting to rivals claiming to offer healthier food. Now, once again, 'McDonald's has a huge image problem in America,' says John Gordon, a restaurant expert at the Pacific Management Consulting Group. This is in part because of its use of frozen 'factory food' packed with preservatives. In 2013 a story about a 14-year-old McDonald's burger that had not rotted received huge coverage. Even Mike Andres, the new boss of the company's American operations, recently asked bemused investors: 'Why do we need to have preservatives in our food?' and then answered himself: 'We probably don't'. McDonald's doesn't seem to be cool anymore, especially among youngsters. Parents say their teenage children have been put off after seeing 'Super-Size Me', a documentary about surviving only on McDonald's food; and 'Food, Inc', another about the corporatization of the food industry; and by reading 'Fast Food Nation: The Dark Side of the All-American Meal'. It is hard to imagine the new McDonald's initiatives getting the reaction Shake Shack got when it opened its first outlet in downtown Chicago in November: for the first two weeks it had long queues of people waiting outside in the freezing cold. A lot of the negative PR that McDonald's gets is the flipside of being the world's biggest and most famous fast-food chain. This has made it the whipping-boy of food activists, labour activists, animal-rights campaigners, and those who simply dislike all things American.

In America it has been the focus of a campaign for fast-food workers and others to get a minimum salary of $15 an hour and the right to unionize. Last month the National Labor Relations Board, a federal agency, released details of 13 complaints against McDonald's and many of its franchisees for violating employees' rights to campaign for better pay and working conditions. The alleged violations relate to threats, surveillance, discrimination, reduced hours, and even sackings of workers who supported the protests. McDonald's contests these charges, while arguing that it is not responsible for its franchisees' labour practices.

Not all the criticism McDonald's gets may be merited—or at least it should be shared more fairly with its peers. However, the company's troubles have begun to attract the attention of activist shareholders, who may prove somewhat harder to brush aside than labour or food activists. In November Jana Partners, an activist fund, took a stake in the firm. Then in December its shares jumped, on rumours that one of the most prominent and determined activists, Bill Ackman, intended to buy a stake and press for a shake-up. McDonald's says it welcomes all investors and is focused on maximizing value for its shareholders.

Even so, Mr Thompson's new strategy needs to deliver results quickly. Mr Ackman's Pershing Square Capital has done well out of its 11% stake in Burger King, because the chain's main shareholder, 3G Capital, has pushed through a drastic cost-cutting programme and a merger with Tim Hortons, a Canadian restaurant group. 'If McDonald's were run like Burger King, the stock would go up a lot,' Mr Ackman mused recently.

It looks like Mr Thompson may soon have to fight on another front. The documental that helped this crisis go horribly wrong McDonald's is a famous fast-food chain around the world. There it has nearly 32,00 local restaurants in more than 100 countries. The first thing anyone will remember after listening to McDonald's is 'BIG Mac'. In 2004 a director called Morgan Spurlock made a documentary movie on McDonald's.

This movie was all about how McDonald's foods affect human body and health condition. He ate McDonald's for 1 month for breakfast, lunch, and dinner. After one month he gained weight, his blood pressure was high, and so on. He increased 5% of his body mass during one week of the month. This movie affected McDonald's reputation very negatively. It decreased the sale of McDonald's by 42 million dollar in the USA. Two overweight girls from New York tried to sue McDonald's for their health condition. After this movie McDonald's tried to change their menu plan. They added healthy and organic foods in their menu. They introduced salads, milkshakes, grilled burgers, and so on. They also changed the environment of their restaurants they painted their restaurants into bright colours to attract the customers.

They started gifting toys with the kid's meal. They added less oily food in their menu such as snack wrap. McDonald's also stopped selling super-size portion in most of their restaurants. They arranged a place for children to play. They also arranged games competitions for school children. This is to show that they are supportive towards the physical activities for the customers.

These are some of the ways McDonald's tried to overcome the negative effects of the Super-size movie on their reputation. They were also successful in making their reputation better as their sales increased every month. In 2008 the global sales of McDonald's increased by 6.9%. Their total revenue in 2008 was 23.5 billion dollar cash returned to the stakeholders were 5.8 billion dollars in 2008.

To sum up it can be said that McDonald's was badly affected by the movie 'Super-Size Me'. That movie represented McDonald's as an unhealthy fast-food chain. But McDonald's effectively carried out damage control exercise by introducing healthy and organic food along with burgers and chips.

McCafe's expansion over the last few years McDonald's has been giving a lot of attention to the expansion of its coffee portfolio, by increasing the presence of McCafe in McDonald's stores. With more than 11,000 stores in the US having McCafe coffee stations, the US customers are already well aware of the brand. However, its popularity is not as widespread as that of Starbucks' coffee or Dunkin? Donuts coffee.

The reason behind this disparity is the perception of McDonald's among US customers. McDonald's has been considered as a typical fast-food chain, which serves on-the-go fast-food items and hamburgers, whereas chains, such as Starbucks, are premium coffee restaurants, with their main focus on coffee service. However, McDonald's has been trying to change this common perception by expanding the number of McCafe coffee stations, as well as by introducing McCafe to retail stores.

In August 2014, McDonald's and Kraft Foods Group announced a deal to expand the manufacture, marketing, and distribution of McDonald's McCafe brand in the US, with effect from early 2015. Shortly after this deal, Kraft Foods entered into a multi-year licensing, manufacturing, and distribution deal with the Vermont based K-Cups maker, Keurig Green Mountain.

After its plans for introducing McCafe in the US, the company decided to expand the reach of its coffee product in Canada, which is its fifth-largest market in terms of number of restaurants. In such a market, where almost 95% of markets are dominated by well-established brands, McCafe might find it difficult to penetrate the Canadian market effectively. Customers will need a strong reason to shift their coffee preferences from the likes of Starbucks and Tim Hortons to McCafe. This might create problems for McDonald's to generate expected sales in the initial years.

However, one of the most prominent reasons for people to shift to McDonald's coffee is that McCafe is slightly cheaper compared to Starbucks' coffee. McCafe's success in Canada might provide a huge boost to the company to expand its McCafe portfolio in its other major markets in Europe and Asia.

McDonald's plans to make another effort to increase its sales in the coming year. The corporation rolls out its plan to reverse the free fall. In addition to removing human antibiotics from its chicken and introducing a bigger, third of a pound burger to its menu, the company's current CEO says it will focus on making food of better quality overall. Despite what they want you to believe, McDonald's was never about the food. There was always better food elsewhere. McDonald's was about the kids, and the parents deserving a 'break'. Now that parents don't have to bring the kids to McDonald's to get the latest Happy Meal toy, I see McDonald's suffering the same fate as the Mc DLT and the fried Hot Apple Pie.

Resultant

The outcome is that customers require not only the product to fulfil their needs but the value to be derived from the product as well as the level of satisfaction gained. Thus it can be said that brands need to work upon creating value and satisfaction to win the customers as it happened with McDonald's in India—segmented the market, targeted, and positioned. Brands need to study the markets thoroughly so as to gain the knowledge about the changing tastes and preferences of the customers and to avoid any decline in the product life cycle. Strategies should be framed in a way that the products occupy the place in the minds of the customers. It is not the brand which is old but the strategies which are renewed. Brands which come up with a bang and make a revival are assumed to occupy the market more efficiently.

Conclusions

Each product has a brand; and every brand has a core value. This core value is shaped by the customers a company attracts. This core value should be unique, different from other products. Once a company understands its core value, it helps the company to create an impressive brand. McDonald's brand was clear before the rice dishes were introduced: an

American style fast-food restaurant. When people go to McDonald's, they expect to enjoy all sorts of high-calorie, greasy, yet so delicious American fast food. This type of food is exactly what people want from McDonald's. The connection between the food it serves and McDonald's brand is strong.

When localizing a product, companies must make sure their new products consistently resonate with their original brand. It is true that some localization will make the product more acceptable for a local culture. McDonald's failure provides a valuable lesson: when a localized product is disconnected from the company's own brand and core value, the customers will be lost, the company is likely to suffer, and the product is all likelihood will fail. Therefore, although innovation is important, reliable market research is also key, some ideas that may work later don't necessarily fit the current market trend as intended.

Case Questions

1. Do you think McDonald's will recover after all the PR scandals and quality issues?

2. Have McDonald's forgotten their recipe of success? What do you think is the main issue in McDonald's fall?

3. Do you think the documentary 'Super-Size Me' was a major reason for this crisis?

20

Ready for Take-off?

A Case Study on Indian E-commerce Industry

Learning Objectives

To understand how the e-commerce industry deals with the requirement of logistics and warehouses. To understand how lack of communication is a huge challenge within the logistical chain. To study how effective the warehouse can account for customer preference to create the right label for business. To understand whether any changes in the economy can affect demand.

Synopsis

The industry has come a long way from the days, to become the backbone of the manufacturing and burgeoning e-commerce industry. The sector is evolving fast, with both the nature of the business and technology driving it, and undergoing dynamic changes. In the face of regulatory and infra-structural challenges, is the warehousing industry-changing gears fast enough to support the growth that the Indian economy. Over a period of time warehousing industry in India has evolved from just brick and mortar shelters for the purpose of storing goods to highly sophisticated stockrooms, where, thanks to advanced tracking mechanism, each con-signment can be tracked on a real-time basis at the click of a button. Not just e-tail, in any industry segment, which deals with physical goods, warehouses play a vital role in the entire value chain from raw material to customer delight.

Indian Business Case Studies. Sandeep Pachpande, Asha Pachpande, and J A Kulkarni, Oxford University Press.
© ASM Group of Institutes, Pune, India 2022. DOI: 10.1093/oso/9780192869371.003.0020

Specifically, in the manufacturing sector, with lean manufacturing becoming the order of the day, a significant part of the functions from scheduling to labelling and packaging are being outsourced to third-party logistics providers. But naturally the warehousing industry is gearing up, with the help of technology, to meet these new requirements. Let us understand the hardship and challenges faced by e-commerce industries.

Warehousing and Logistics Will Be the Key Challenges for Online Firms Joining the Grocery Retail Party

Global e-commerce giant Amazon recently piloted its grocery delivery process, branded Kirana Now, in Bengaluru wherein one could place orders via mobile phone. Home-bred Flipkart plans to go down the same path in the second half of this year. The market for food and grocery is set to get more competitive with players such as 24x7 Fresh, Pepper Tap, Falsabzi, Justshop24 throwing their hats into the ring.

Though small and highly disintegrated at present, online grocery retailing in India is growing at 30% annually and is expected to touch Rs 270 crore by 2019 (according to a Ken Research report), thanks to the surge in the number of players operating in the industry. 'This is the "mother of all categories" in terms of size and the repetitive nature of the need. Grocery shopping is also the biggest pain point for the consumer,' says K Ganesh, a serial entrepreneur, and promoter in online grocery store Big Basket

Globally, grocery retailing—which comprise 60–70% of traditional brick-and-mortar-retailing—seems to be the next frontier for online firms to conquer because that segment is still relatively untapped. A new study, 'e-commerce Supply Chain Insights in Groceries and Consumer Packaged Goods in the United States (February 2015)', by Amitabh Sinha of University of Michigan and Paul Wetzel of Willard Bishop (with research assistance by Manqi Li, Jianyu Liu), shows that even in the US, e-commerce in the grocery and consumer packaged goods (CPG) sector is lagging. It currently only accounts for about 3% of total sales. But the authors expect the sector to grow rapidly across all e-commerce retailers, including pure-play and brick-and mortar-stores. 'Brick and mortar retailers that also have e-commerce operations are moving toward an Omni-channel strategy,' the report says.

While the potential is obvious, selling groceries online is a bigger challenge than any other category, given the complexities of supply chain management, logistics, relatively low margins, and the consumer need for quick fulfilment. 'This is not a game for angel investors and early-stage VCs—margins are low and scale is important. Since 2012 there were 40 companies of which only three have managed to raise money and 30 of them have shut shop,' adds Ganesh.

Figures in %

	Store inventory				DC* inventory		Dark store
	Van delivery	In-vehicle pickup	In-store pickup	Parcel	Van Delivery	Parcel	Van Delivery
Fee and order size	×	×	×	×	×	×	×
Warehouse occupancy					14	11.2	
Store shopping labour	21.8	28.9	27.1	17.9			22
Store accupancy	17.4	24.5	22.9	9.5			
Supply expenses				25		50.4	
Delivery expenses	27				39.5		33.4
Share of direct ABs**	66.1	53.4	50	52.4	53.5	61.6	55.5

Notes: Under the store models, retailers still have many of the normal brick & mortar expenses to move product through the warehouse and store, even before the incremental e-commerce activities begin. Under the DC programmes, there are no store-level expenses. *DC: Distribution centre; **ABC-Activity based costing

Figure 20.1 Cost drivers in grocery e-commerce fulfilment

Eye on Stock Management

Managing inventory is the most challenging task for any player in this space, especially if it follows an inventory-led business model. Delivering on the promise of reaching perishable items in the mint-fresh condition is easier said than done. Big Basket has tied up with around 400 suppliers such as large FMCG companies like P&G, Unilever, Kellogg, institutional farmers, importers, and aggregators to source products that they wish to sell to the final consumer. Hence, it is critical to hold small inventory as more inventory means more storage space and probably more wastage. On the other hand, too little inventory may mean falling short of consumer expectations.

But how do you determine the ideal inventory amount? This will require forecasting and a well-oiled turnaround mechanism. Technology is the biggest facilitator in this. 'If you plan and rotate the inventory with the help of technology, you can ensure minimum capital compared to a brick and mortar stores where the minimum holding period for inventory is between 25 and 30 days,' says Rajiv Tetviya, co-founder, Green cart. Green cart stocks gourmet and grocery products based on daily and monthly requirements.

Big Basket also manages its orders with the help of algorithms that factor in sales rates, seasonality of products, suppliers' frequency of delivery, their performance in the past, and so on. Even order placements are forecasted with the help of algorithms, which can be adjusted to factor in variables such as promotional offers or a new launch, both of which can trigger changes in consumer demand patterns. Co-founder Vipul Parekh says the firm operates with 10-day inventory, with perishable items like fruits and vegetables having a smaller window of a day and a half.

Big Basket operates in Bangalore, Mumbai, Hyderabad, Pune, and Chennai and has a warehouse in each of these cities. The suppliers deliver at the centralized distribution centre where inventory is held and delivered to the transhipment points or customer's premises directly. The company has invested around Rs 30–40 crore per warehouse and around 20% of its investment is towards technology.

Now consider ZopNow, an online grocery store based in Bangalore, which has gone through a shift in its business model. The company used to manage its inventory in the past but switched to a tie-up with offline retailer Hyper City. 'We save on rentals of warehouse and other associated capital costs,' says Mukesh Singh, CEO, ZopNow. Since it delivers from stores located in the central part of a city, its shipment costs have gone down dramatically. Almost 40% of its orders are now delivered in less than 90 minutes from the time it takes the order; in some cases, the delivery time is as low as 30 minutes. 'It opens up the entire Omni-channel route for us where offline and online businesses can work together to pass on the benefit to the consumer,' adds Singh.

The company plans to step into Pune, Mumbai, and Hyderabad in some time.

On its part, Local Banya employs a mix of just in time (JIT) sourcing and warehousing. Fast-moving items such as staples are stocked in warehouses as there is a steady and measurable demand for them. For other items, it uses JIT, procuring things from vendors and suppliers on an as-per-need basis. 'It is not possible to warehouse everything. So we have to employ this mix efficiently,' says Karan Mehrotra, co-founder, Local Banya.

Keeping It Fresh

It is important to ensure perishable items reach the customer without delay or damage. As soon as an item of food is delivered to Big Basket's warehouse, it goes for a quality check, cleaning of debris and mud, segregation of dead leaves, etc., followed by packaging and labelling before finally hitting the shelves. More than 80% of its orders are for fresh produce. 'You need to innovate and think of solutions that would work in the Indian market. That means looking for local suppliers for equipment, products, and so on,' adds Parekh. Another new entrant, Falsabzi, has earmarked an investment of Rs 100 crore in the next five years. 'Our operating margin will be 30 percent and rest we want to pass on to the consumer,' says Rajesh Gupta, chairman, RSND Group.

Some players have started branding products that they sell. 'Any company in this space has to build its brand of staples and other items but it will require deep sourcing expertise on where and how to source the best products at a competitive price and consistent quality,' adds Ganesh. Meanwhile, Pepper Tap, an on-demand hyperlocal grocery delivery company, claims that 90% of its transactions come through the mobile. Pepper Tap connects directly with the local vendors and supermarkets and promises delivery in two hours. It is working on a marketplace model. 'We didn't want to incur a lot of capital cost involved in setting up or manning a warehouse,' says Navneet Singh, co-founder, Pepper Tap.

But that has its challenges. 'A major constraint in the store pick models is reduced margins since the company will have to share it with stores they operate with,' adds Parekh. To get around this, Big Basket is tying up with local kirana stores in Bangalore to supply the inventory to local stores. In this model, the company has more control over the supply quality and the availability of products.

People Movement and Logistics

Technology can also help in picking, packing, and delivering orders accurately. In the cold chain facility at Green cart's warehouse, employees follow a specific code of conduct to ensure there is a minimum human touch involved in the entire process of handling fresh produce. So far the company has invested more than Rs 50 lakh in its cold chain. 'Human processes and their integration with technology have improved productivity for Green cart by almost three times,' claims Tetviya. The company works on the 'relay race principle' where it takes less than three minutes to process an order. At Big Basket, the warehouse is designed in a manner that minimizes the path a picker has to cover, thus saving on time. It has around 400 vans to manage its operations.

Green cart has drawn up a service level agreement with set standards that all its suppliers have to adhere to. The onus for a product past its expiry date lies with the supplier. Big Basket is working with a few recycling companies to dispose of organic waste. Technology plays a crucial role in the last mile as well. It is now working to introduce a 'track your exact time of delivery' feature. Most of the ZopNowvans are also GPS tagged and orders are geo-fenced to give an insight into the time it takes to deliver, helping it to map the delivery processes accurately. 'The average delivery time was about 95 to 100 minutes and with technology, in some places, we have been able to reduce it to 60 minutes,' says Singh of Pepper Tap.

Outcome

India's growth in online grocery retailing due to Global e-commerce in spite of facing inventory and warehousing challenges is remarkable. Though the requirement of forecasting and a well-oiled turnaround mechanism is needed and technology is the biggest facilitator in this. Various organizations are coming up with various models to make smooth flow of inventory and in all this process technology is providing an add on advantage to all the organizations with all trending features to ensure delivery of product takes place on time and with accuracy

Conclusions

E-commerce industry is definitely a boon to Indian economy but at the same time certain challenges and obstacles with respect to logistics and warehousing are not allowing the industry to go ahead and take country's economy to the next level. So it is important that these obstacles and challenges should be tackled and the customers should be given a hassle-free service which will really have a positive overall impact on the business of these industries.

Case Questions

1. As per the growing business of the e-commerce industry do you think that warehousing and logistics have become a challenge and if yes, can you suggest strategies to overcome the same?

2. How should perishable products treated by such companies to ensure that customers get such products on time and without damaging its perishable nature of the product?

3. Can the role of technology in this sector be a boon?

Lightning Source UK Ltd.
Milton Keynes UK
UKHW021831260123
416031UK00010B/122